Start Your
RESTAURANT
Career

Other Entrepreneur Pocket Guides include

Start Your Real Estate Career

Start Your
RESTAURANT
Career

Entrepreneur Press and
Heather Heath Dismore

Editorial Director: Jere L. Calmes
Advisory Editor: Jack Savage
Cover Design: Beth Hansen-Winter
Production and Composition: Eliot House Productions

This publication is designed to provide accurate and authoritative information in regard to the subject matter covered. It is sold with the understanding that the publisher is not engaged in rendering legal, accounting or other professional services. If legal advice or other expert assistance is required, the services of a competent professional person should be sought.

Library of Congress Cataloging-in-Publication Data
    Dismore, H. (Heather).
       Start your restaurant career/by Heather Heath Dismore.
       p.   cm.
       ISBN: 1-59918-000-6 (9781599180007: alk. paper)
       1. Restaurant management. I. Entrepreneur Press. II. Title.
    TX911.3.M27D582 2006
    647.95068—dc22   2005034878

Printed in Canada
12 11 10 09 08 07 06   10 9 8 7 6 5 4 3 2 1

Contents

Chapter 1

All About the Restaurant Business 1

Dedication

To my husband, Andrew, without whom this book would not be possible. You're the most amazing chef and foodservice professional I know.

Acknowledgments

Thank you so much to the team at Entrepreneur Press—Jere Calmes, Karen Thomas, and Jen Dorsey—for the opportunity to write this book. Your endless patience and support during the process have been truly wonderful. A big thank you to Karen Billipp for shepherding this book through the editorial process.

Thanks to all the industry professionals who graciously agreed to participate in the research for this book: Chef Andrew Dismore, Chef Rob "RC" Corliss, Chef Hans Schadler, Steve Price, Michael Garvey, Dave Mazzorana, Karen Fox, Rick Enos, Chef Jordan Holcomb, Pete Mervis, and Amanda McDermitt.

Thanks also to my incredible family and friends for their patience and support.

Preface

Work can, and should be, fulfilling. Most people spend as much time at work as they do at home with their families. In the restaurant business, people spend more waking hours at the restaurant than with their families or friends. While a job won't satisfy most people in the same way that their personal lives do, it should make them happy and fulfilled while they're at work. The key to being satisfied at work is finding a career that matches your personality and goals.

Understanding Your Personality

Figuring out who you are is essential. For many, it's a lifelong journey. As you go along, you figure out things about yourself. You find things you're passionate about. You find things that you can't deal with, and still other things that leave you

totally lukewarm. Knowing who you are (and what you like and dislike) can help you find a career that makes you happy for the long haul. Pay particular attention to Chapter 2: About You, and Chapter 5: The Working Environment, to see how you might fit in with the culture and daily life of the restaurant business.

Setting Goals for Yourself

Goals are your lifelong, big picture to-do list. Everyone needs goals. Goals help you figure out where you want to go and are the first steps in constructing a plan to get there. Maybe you have a big goal of owning your own restaurant someday. Break that goal up into smaller, incremental ones that you need to achieve on your way to meeting the larger goal.

Maybe your goal list looks something like this:

- Get a job working in a restaurant kitchen.
- Learn every station in the kitchen.
- Understand the sanitation systems in the restaurant.
- Go to culinary school.
- Understand how the front of the house works in a restaurant.
- Understand restaurant financial information, including how to purchase food, cost menus, and figure out labor percentages.
- Own my own restaurant.

Each of those goals can be broken down into many smaller goals. Keep going, and pretty soon, you've created a plan for yourself and a map to your new career.

This book is a shortcut to helping you figure out if you're interested in pursuing a career in the restaurant business and creating a plan to get there. Take a look at Chapter 3 to see what education and training you need to pursue different jobs. Chapter 4 gives you details on what jobs exist in the industry, how you get them, and how much you can expect to make.

Deciding on a Career

You've taken a great first step toward researching a career in the restaurant business just by picking up this book. In it, I give you tons of information about what it's really like to work in a restaurant day in and day out, year after year. I help you take a look at different career options to see what might fit you best. And I tell you how to get the training you need to pursue a particular career. If you're still not sure that this business is the right one for you, make sure to see Chapter 6 for great tips on trying it out without committing your whole life to it.

Staying Motivated in Your Career

In any career, it's sometimes tough to stay focused on the long-term goal, especially once the excitement of learning a new skill wears off. The restaurant business is no different. But in this book, I help you stay energized. In a nutshell, the secret is continuing to learn, continuing to innovate, and never being satisfied with "good enough." Chapters 8, 9, and 10 give you information on getting the job, staying ahead of the curve, and ultimately, going out on your own.

All About the
Restaurant Business

on the day of the week and also does all the baking for the employee cafeteria at Google. The Creamery, as the locals know it, has two locations in Palo Alto, one near the Stanford University campus and the other near the border of Menlo Park and Palo Alto. Despite the close proximity of the two restaurants (three minutes by car), they serve two different markets.

Being a leader and general manager (GM) in the restaurant business came very naturally to Dave. At 19, he was the youngest GM in McDonald's history at the time. He was brought up through the corporate ladder, rather than pursuing an industry-specific degree. He knows a handful of restaurant professionals who pursued degrees but believes that most people still "fall into" the business. He notes, "People get through programs without really learning enough, no matter what kind of program they're in. A degree doesn't reflect your talent or your work ethic. Many people without the degree do really, really well in the business." He points out that a prospective employee's experience and work history can tell you a lot about the person, adding, "The degree doesn't tell you what they can do, how well they know the industry, etc. It tells you they have a degree."

He concedes that when starting out, "You might want to have [a degree] just to be competitive." But ultimately he thinks it's more important to be generally well educated and well read, rather than specifically "schooled" in the hospitality industry. As a leader in your restaurant, he thinks you should "be able to converse on a variety of topics" with your diners.

After 30 years, Dave still has fun. As he says, "You get rewards and feedback everyday. It's immediate gratification, every day, every meal. At the end of the day you know how you did, and what you can work on." He also finds the business to be a great creative outlet. He gets to figure out how to solve a great variety of challenges and loves that every day is different.

He enjoys working at his current restaurant because he feels it's part of the community. With more regular customers, you get to know the guests well. He says, " [Here] you're feeding your neighbors, friends, and family. [We're] getting back to that sense of community."

Dave sees a positive future for the restaurant business. He sees dining out becoming more entertainment than necessity, noting, "It's expensive to go out to dinner *and* a movie. Dining can be the full entertainment for the evening." And he recognizes that busy families with both parents working often feel too busy cook. "Many people don't have the skills to cook even basic comfort food. Many more options for prepared foods will be available in grocery stores, even in large national chains."

For the would-be restaurateur, Dave says, "Work hard, learn the financial side of the business, no matter what, as soon as you can,

whenever you can. Understand the inside and outside of the financials of the restaurant business. Educate yourself, by buying books,
going to school, whatever works for you. Learn how this business
works, and understand what your role is in affecting the money.
Don't open your own place until you know it inside and out."

■ ■ ■

The restaurant industry is white hot. In 2005, restaurant
sales are expected to increase almost 5 percent over the
previous year to $476 billion, or close to $1.3 billion in sales
each and every day.

For those looking to get started in the business, opportunity
abounds in every segment, from hourly to salaried positions,
from fast food to fine dining, in every job from dishwashers to
general managers. Currently, the restaurant industry is the
country's largest private-sector employer, with 12.2 million
people (9 percent of all working Americans). Experts predict
that number will grow to 14 million by 2015, thus creating
nearly 300,000 new jobs each and every year. One in four
adults got their very first job in the restaurant business. And
an astonishing 42 percent of adults have worked in restaurants at one time or another.

Perhaps the most exciting thing about the industry is that
you need very little in the way of education or training to get

started. Most restaurants offer some sort of training. And even if you're already working in another field, you could try out the business through part-time employment. Nearly 40 percent of restaurant employees work part time. With the right attitude, you can get started today in this growing and exciting industry.

How the Industry Developed

Taverns connected to inns have existed for centuries. They operated like a modern day bed and breakfast; a meal was served with a set menu, at a specific time, at the host's table. Dining a la carte, or "from a menu," as is done in restaurants today, originated in France, in the mid- to late-17th-century. The number of restaurants exploded as a direct result of the French Revolution. As wealth was redistributed to the growing middle class, people chose to spend some of it "eating like kings," which to them meant choosing their meals from menus. The first use of the word *restaurant* was to describe a product that was believed to "restore health." *Restaurateurs* were people who knew how to make these restorative concoctions. While restaurants are still paying attention to nutrition, it's only part of the story today.

Trends over Time

In this country, restaurants grew around travel routes and in urban centers. As people traveled from town to town, they needed lodging and food along the way. The cuisine was typical of the home cooking of the region, and menus were limited. In urban areas, true menu-based restaurants grew to meet the needs of the growing middle and upper classes. As people worked further away from their homes, they were less likely to be able to return for a noon meal. Restaurants and lunch counters began to fill those needs. Even in the 1950s, most people rarely ate in restaurants. When they did, it was a special event, usually on a holiday or vacation. Today, restaurants account for 46.7 percent of Americans' food spending dollar (compared to 25 percent in 1955), and that number is going up. Estimates indicate that by the 2010, Americans will be spending 53 cents out of every food dollar in restaurants, rather than grocery stores. As incomes go up, people spend less time in the kitchen and more time in restaurants.

Dining as "Eater-tainment"

Restaurants aren't just a convenience today. For many people, eating in a restaurant is still an event, an event that occurs more often than in previous generations, but an event nonetheless. People are often looking for more than just a quality meal at a value price. They're also looking at the meal as what industry people call "eater-tainment." Many are stretching the meal out longer to savor more, but smaller, courses, in the Spanish tapas tradition. They are lingering over different wines, an after dinner drink, or a gourmet coffee. They are sharing desserts. And they're doing so in increasingly eclectic and ethnic settings. Whether it's a Brazilian churrascaria (where servers come to your table with knives and a skewer, on which are speared various kinds of roasted meats), or a special table set aside in the wine cellar, more restaurants are looking to deliver an experience to diners, rather than just a meal.

Industry Segments

Everyone eats many times a day. And that's good news for us! The restaurant business can capture a diner once, twice, maybe three times a day at a variety of different venues. Here's a look at the industry segments where consumers choose to spend their restaurant dollars every single day.

QSR (Fast Food)

QSR stands for *Quick Service Restaurant* in restaurant lingo (fast food restaurants to the rest of the world). Big names in this segment include McDonalds, Burger King, Wendy's, Kentucky Fried Chicken, Taco Bell, Dairy Queen, Subway, and a host of regional competitors that are near and dear to the hearts of those who know them. In theory, diners get a quality meal, at a relatively inexpensive price, that's consistent at each and every restaurant in the chain. Often, these restaurants have a drive-through or pickup window to make getting your meal even easier.

Many of these restaurants are franchises, meaning they're owned by individuals, but must follow strict rules and policies set up by the national company to ensure that diners experience

the same food and service at every restaurant that bears its name. The franchise owners pay the company a fee. For more details about the pros and cons of franchising a restaurant, see Chapter 10.

Fast Casual

Fast casual refers to a new breed of restaurant that fits somewhere between fast food and casual restaurants, hence the name. These restaurants offer speedy dining, but more sophisticated menu options. Orders are made as the customer requests them, not before. Often diners order their meals from a restaurant employee, who handles their entrée as they move down a cold or hot table full of add-ons or condiments. Diners are able to customize their meals and make them their own by choosing fresh ingredients bursting with flavor. Then, they enjoy their meals in more upscale settings than the average fast food restaurant. Typically, these restaurants have moveable tables with moveable chairs, rather than chairs and tables bolted together and to the floor as in many fast food restaurants. Examples of fast casual restaurants are Chipotle, Baja Fresh, Panera Bread, and Quizno's.

Family Dine

Family dine restaurants were the first restaurants to make it big in this country. They are the "sit-down" restaurants that dominated the restaurant scene for the 50 years following

World War II. Family-friendly, familiar entrée items (everything from spaghetti to meatloaf, turkey manhattans to fried chicken) graced the menus. As the American public craved more variety and more ethnic flavors, some restaurants focused on filling particular needs. Rather than keeping everything on their menus, they focused on a particular meal (like breakfast) or a type of cuisine (maybe Italian fare or seafood). Denny's, buffet restaurants like Golden Corral, and cafeterias fall into this category.

Casual

Casual restaurants offer a variety of menu options, often centered on a theme of some sort. The theme could be ethnic (as in the case of PF Chang's China Bistro), cuisine based (like Joe's Crab Shack), or even geographic (Outback Steakhouse). Other examples of casual restaurants are Applebee's, Don Pablo's Mexican Kitchen, Romano's Macaroni Grill, The Cheesecake Factory, and Olive Garden. These restaurants may or may not have a bar. Some may have a limited bar, perhaps just beer or wine, while others have a bartender and fully-stocked bar.

Pizza

Pizza is its own market segment (not to say that other restaurants don't serve pizza, of course) because there's such variation within the segment. Many pizza places focus on delivery without customer seating. Some focus on entertainment (like

Chuck E. Cheese's), and still others are full restaurants with bands on weekends.

Fine Dining

Fine dining restaurants traditionally offer impeccable service, white tableclothes (although this is no longer a must), a wine list, and an often-changing menu. Typically, they have a dress code and an ambiance to match. Men may be required to wear jackets and ties, or jeans may not be permitted. A meal often consists of many courses, rather than just an entrée.

Many require reservations, and some even have specific seating times, meaning that they seat the entire restaurant twice an evening, serving all the guests the same menu. While it may sound confining, restaurants like the French Laundry in California's Napa Valley and Bouley in New York are among the top tier in the world. Many of these high-end restaurants have web sites with menus and pictures of the interiors posted. Here are a few to check out:

- Bouley in New York (www.bouley.net)
- French Laundry in Napa Valley, California (www.frenchlaundry.com)
- Morimoto in Philadelphia, Pennsylvania (www.morimotorestaurant.com)
- Boulevard in San Francisco, California (www.boulevardrestaurant.com)

- Chez Panisse in Berkeley, California (www.chezpanisse.com)
- El Bulli in Spain (www.elbulli.com)
- Tru in Chicago, Illinois (www.trurestaurant.com)
- Gabriel's in Highwood, Illinois (www.egabriels.com/intro.html)

Bar/Tavern

Bars and taverns were the first restaurants, and they are still among the most popular. Whether it's your local neighborhood place "where everybody knows your name" or a chain, bars do a booming business. While they make most of their money on alcohol sales, their food dollars are increasing. More bars are offering better food, often referred to as "pub grub," as a point of distinction, trying to get diners to choose their establishment over another. Many chains are getting into the action and doing well (Dave and Busters, the Fox and the Hound, and Irish pub concepts, Fado and Claddagh).

Contracted Food Service

Contracted food service is a fancy name given to restaurants that operate within other businesses, like food service in a student union building on a college campus, the employee cafeteria in an office building, or the food areas in a stadium or arena. An increasing number of employers are offering these amenities to employees in order to keep them "on campus," or closer to work, while still offering a variety of dining choices. Big names in the business include Aramark and Sedexho.

Catering

Catering offers a unique challenge. Some restaurants cater from their restaurant kitchens, whereas others operate separate kitchens geared toward catering. Still other companies choose to focus on catering and forego the traditional restaurant setting altogether. Some cater at their facilities, usually banquet halls (called *on-premise* catering); others specialize in *off-premise* catering, coming to specific locations, perhaps your parent's backyard for your wedding reception. Catering offers different challenges than a restaurant because you often feed a large number of people in a short time. As a caterer, you work out the puzzle that is the business.

Hotels and Resorts

Hotels and resorts offer a wide range of dining options. In fact, restaurants are the largest employer in the tourism segment. From banquets to room service, from coffee shops to oceanfront fine dining venues, variety is the true spice of life in this industry segment. And because many hotels and resorts are owned by larger companies or corporations, they often offer benefits that independent restaurants can't match, like complimentary hotel rooms and paid transfers to exotic locations.

Why Size (and Geography) Matter

The restaurant industry is made up mostly of small businesses. In fact, seven out of ten restaurants and bars are independent (that is, not part of a chain of any sort) with fewer than 20 employees. You can get great experience working for both small and large restaurant companies because with small independents, you get more responsibility and flexibility. With larger companies, you tend to get more systems to help you run your business. Some sizes are more successful than others in certain areas.

Here's a brief list of how geography affects restaurants in different areas.

- In larger metro areas, there is usually a mix of large and small companies.
- In some quaint communities, large companies (i.e., fast food) are prohibited.
- Some geographic areas have more of a cooking culture in the home, which results in fewer restaurants overall.
- Downtown (near business districts) areas may be prime for breakfast and lunch, but not dinner.

There's room for everyone—if you're smart and talented.

State of the Industry

Is it fast-paced, changing rapidly, or staid, or resisting change? All of those. It really depends on how you look at it. The day-to-day work is fast paced and resistant to change. It's still feeding people, making the most out of your opportunity to give them an experience they'll want to return for. But how restaurateurs achieve their goals is changing. Overall, response to guests' preferences gets better and faster every year. As the guest becomes more savvy and demanding, restaurants are challenged to either improve their products and service or die.

Day-to-Day Pace

Day-to-day work in the restaurant business is hectic, frenetic, and kinetic. You prep and stock for hours, then deplete that stock and start all over again. If you're a shift worker in the business, you'll be on your feet for the entire shift. You'll be cooking entrees, preparing salads, cleaning glassware and silverware, serving dessert, talking to guests, answering the phone, sweeping behind the bar, and performing innumerable other tasks. If you're a manager, you'll get to do many of these things, too, all while you're making sure that everyone else is doing their jobs and all the guests are beyond satisfied. You'll get to sit down after all the guests are gone (or before they arrive if you open the restaurant for the day), make sure all the money is counted and secured properly, food orders are placed for the next day, all trash has been removed from the premises, all equipment is shut down, and various other details are taken care of. It's crazy, but above all, it's fun.

At the end of the day, the restaurant business is feeding people, lots of people. People have more choices than ever, with the opportunity to eat at any hour of the day. They can choose from almost limitless menus items, service levels, and ambiance. That variety means lots of opportunity for you, the soon-to-be restaurant professional.

Who Thrives in the Industry?

Athletes and entertainers have something in common with successful restaurant professionals. They understand that you practice and rehearse (in the restaurant business prep and train) for the moment when the whistle blows, the curtain goes up, or the doors open. All three groups are dedicated to doing their best and competing, whether the prize is a game, a packed house, or a strong client base. They all feel the rush of physical and mental exertion as the game, show, or shift begins. The whirlwind calms, and all celebrate the post-game, post-show, or post-shift festivities. In the restaurant business, half the fun is that rush. The other half is the desire to make people happy and ensure that they have a good time. As a restaurant professional, people will look to you to make the fun happen. You have the opportunity to take that expectation and blow your customers away.

People who like instant gratification are particularly well suited to this business. I have a longtime friend in the business who thinks it's the ideal industry for people with ADHD, because they can focus on what interests them and get instant positive strokes. While that's far from a scientifically proven fact, it does underscore the fact that you can be successful in this business today, right now. Your success is truly in your own hands.

The "Right" People

Anyone who has a positive outlook, an upbeat personality, and isn't afraid of hard work can be extremely successful in this business. Take a look at Chapter 2 for details on how to match your personality with this exciting industry. Because on-the-job training is a must, an expensive degree isn't necessary. Ultimately, to get to the highest levels in the business, you'll probably need a degree (or maybe two or three), but you can have a successful career without one. And more importantly, you'll need to "crave" making people happy. It must be a passion for you.

Benefits

This business is one of the few that is truly entrepreneurial. Many restaurants operate within corporate guidelines, but many leave room for innovation and experimentation. And it's an industry that's growing at a steady, strong rate. People gotta eat and more and more often, they're doing it in restaurants.

In this dynamic business, you can

- work anywhere in the world.
- work as many, or as few, hours a week as you want.
- work a variety of shifts.
- get a job today.
- learn new skills or techniques each and every day.
- work your way into management, regardless of your education level.

Sacrifices

In a nutshell, you sacrifice quite a bit of your free time, but if you enjoy your job, it's not so tough. If you have a family, you'll sacrifice time with them. It's likely that you will be working on holidays, weekends, and birthdays. More specifically, you'll sacrifice traditional time with family. But if family is a priority for you, you'll find other time to spend with them.

For example, when our oldest daughter was little, my husband was a *chef de cuisine* (meaning he was in charge of a single restaurant on a property with several restaurants) at a fine dining restaurant in a national hotel chain. He worked virtually every night, and a good chunk of the day as well. But we worked out a system for him to spend time with our daughter. He worked until 11:00 P.M. or midnight, and then he'd come home and sleep until I went in to work at around 8:00 A.M. Before I left, he'd get up and spend several hours with our daughter before taking her to daycare at noon. He'd go into work around 1:00 P.M. or so. Many working parents don't get that kind of time with their kids, so it's definitely possible to have healthy family relationships and still be part of the restaurant world. You just have to be creative in figuring out how to balance it all. We also made sure that everyone in the family had one day off each week together, and agreed to spend it doing something together.

The Bottom Line

As with just about any industry, the restaurant business uses several key numbers to rate how successful the business is.

Two of the biggest numbers are food cost percentages and labor percentages. In a nutshell, restaurateurs compare their sales figures to the amount of money they spend on food and labor. So if a restaurant's sales are $100,000 in a month and the operator spends $10,000 on food, the food cost percentage is 10 percent of the total sales. (FYI: I'm using nice round numbers here. Very few, if any restaurants actually run a 10 percent food cost percentage, but you get the idea.) The same principle applies to labor percentages. If the restaurant's sales are $100,000 in a month and the operator spends $20,000 on wages, salaries, and benefits, the labor percentage is 20 percent.

Together these numbers (plus beverage costs) are called *prime costs*. Ultimately you have to keep your prime costs within 60 to 68 percent of your sales range. If you get to 70 percent or higher, you won't have enough left to pay the rent, operating costs, and other overhead costs. Of course, this explanation of these key figures is very simplified. For a more detailed look into how to figure out the actual costs associated with running a restaurant, check out *Running a Restaurant For Dummies*, by Michael Garvey, Andrew Dismore, and me, Heather Dismore (John Wiley and Sons, 2004).

Make More Money

The old adage, "You make more money buying than selling," is definitely true in the restaurant business. Your goal as a restaurateur is to keep more of every dollar that comes in, and you do that by watching how quickly the money goes out. Buy your products right, and you're a long way toward profitability.

The only money that comes in the door is from people buying items on the menu. At a certain point, you can only charge so much for a grilled chicken salad because people are used to paying certain prices for certain types of food in a particular setting. Sure, you can increase the number of grilled chicken salads you sell by getting more people in the door, but you still can only charge so much for each salad.

In order to be profitable, you need to spend less to sell that chicken salad to your customers. One major way to do that is by watching how much you pay for your chicken, your lettuce, your cheese, your salad dressing, and so on. The rate that money goes out the door is entirely dependent on how you spend it. Successful restaurateurs don't buy "cheap" products; instead, they buy products "right."

Here are a few examples of how restaurant buyers weigh decisions in order to run a cost-effective food program. They consider

- the cost of producing products from scratch vs. using some prepared, convenience foods. (Should they make their own croutons vs. buy them already made?)
- buying items in bulk vs. carrying too much unused inventory. (Sure they got a great deal on ten cases of white wine, but if no one drinks it, what kind of deal is it?)

- the benefits of entering into exclusive agreements to get better pricing. (If a buyer carries beer from only one distributor in order to save 12 cents a bottle, swing a deal to get free neon bar signs, coasters, tap handles, and the like.)
- the quality of the products they're buying compared to the expectations of their customers. (If you advertise that you use only Black Angus beef, prime quality steaks, or fresh seafood, your customers expect that.)

The Future

The restaurant business is shaped almost exclusively by consumer demand. Sometimes restaurants respond to the demand (advertising 30-minute lunch specials), and other times they create the demand (mass marketing of the big burrito by Chipotle, for example).

A few restaurant-relevant demographic trends provided by the National Restaurant Association are:

- The nation's baby boomers will continue to drive growth in consumer spending. The number of Americans between 50 and 64, currently 16 percent of the population, will grow to 19 percent by 2010. This aging population may cause a shift or an expansion in dining hours. As these people retire, they won't be swayed by the convenience of QSR. As they have more free time, they'll spend it in eater-tainment settings, in sit-down restaurants of all types. And because they have more experience in restaurants, they will have a higher expectation for quality in segments in the market.

- America is continuing its trend toward diversity. In 2003, Hispanics made up 13 percent of the population, up from 6 percent in 1980. By 2010, experts estimate that Hispanics will represent 14.6 percent of the U.S. population. As society becomes more diverse, it will be exposed to different flavors and ingredients. As these flavors and ingredients become more familiar, customers will respond positively to them on menus. Ingredients that seem obscure now will become commonplace as our growing ethnic communities bring demand for their indigenous cuisine.
- High-income households are more common than ever. After adjusting for inflation, 25 percent of households today have incomes of $75,000 or more, compared to 14.2 percent in 1982. More households are able to spend more money on eating out than every before.

Some dining trends in progress include:

- *Dashboard dining.* So many meals are literally consumed in the car, on the go on the dashboard. Families are busier, more on the go than ever. The timing of family meals is often based on highly scheduled lives, at least a night or two each week. The family goes from activity A to B to C and on the way, it's going to choke down a meal in the car.

- *Multi-stop dining.* Among the dashboard diners, it's becoming common for the family to visit different restaurants in the same meal period, so the parents may consume food from one QSR, while the kids eat from another.

- *Curbside service.* Once a staple only in high-density urban areas, many suburban casual restaurants are now offering carryout service. Call ahead, place your order, pull up into a special reserved parking area, and restaurant employees bring your food to you. People want quality food to serve their families, and they want it quick.

- *Discerning palates without the cooking skills to match.* Today diners are increasingly food savvy. They know what they want food to taste like but don't know how (or don't want to spend the time) to really cook. They look to restaurants to meet this challenge.

Some important emerging trends are:

- *Regional foods.* A certain subset of diner is no longer satisfied with basic ethnic foods; they want even more specialized regional ethnic foods. They want their food with a story. They don't want just Latin food; they want Cuban, or something Vera Cruz. They're looking at Vietnamese, Thai, Malaysian, or Indonesian, for example. Diners are searching for authenticity in cuisine. (Contrary to popular belief, not all Asian food is flavored with soy sauce.) More diners want to experience the culture and the flavor of true regional cuisine.

- *Wholesomeness.* Obesity is not a new problem in America and experts think that the rising rate of childhood obesity just might get Americans to stand up and actually make long-term, healthy changes in their diets. As people look at eating healthier (not just low fat, low carb, or other trends of the week), more will start looking at the quality of their food from a nutritional point of view. They'll be inspecting nutrition labels for "Frankenfood," or chemical additives and other modified food ingredients. They may not be looking for "organic," "free range," or other buzz words, but expect to see a trend back toward real food ingredients.

- *Concern over safety of foods.* As the media whips up a frenzy over safe food supplies, expect an ongoing reaction to concerns about unsafe beef (mad cow disease or e.coli) and seafood (rising levels of mercury and other toxins). Some restaurants respond by working more closely with local growers, artisan cheese makers, and bakers. This supply seems to feel more fresh and natural to consumers. It's recognized as better quality than "big corporate food."

- *Molecular gastronomy.* This marriage of food science and culinary arts takes into account the modern understanding of the way that the brain interprets smell and taste. It challenges traditional perceptions and customs about what makes food appetizing, what flavor combinations work, and why. It also is the study of heat transfer at the molecular level to study the "perfect" way to cook something. You can find its influence in the mainstream of cuisine and on the fringes in what some people call *mad scientist food*. Chefs use flavored foams (yes, it looks like foamy hand soap), flavored paper and ink with printouts of pictures of food (instead of the actual food), and presentation techniques like levitation.

About
You

In addition to the normal GM duties, Garvey sees his role in a more global way, "I run one of the most famous and longest-running restaurants in New York, I am also a caretaker. If I do my job correctly, this restaurant will certainly outlive me."

Despite his amazing success, Garvey started in the business accidentally. He says, "I never understood why my friends wanted to work as bussers or waiters. Forget the long hours and hard work (I was used to that already), I watched them navigate minefields of difficult customers . . . and they seemed to enjoy it! Then, out of economic educational necessity, I picked up a job as a waiter at a Caesar's resort. I could not believe it, but I did love it. I actually got off making a difficult table happy. When the feeling didn't wear off, I knew I wanted to pursue this as a career."

Once he committed to the business, he formulated his plan. He worked as a bartender and did some time in the kitchen. Then he decided if he was going to make this a true career, he needed to educate himself about the restaurant business. He determined that he should "forgo the better short-term money in service and start learning how to actually run a restaurant by getting into management. "I headed back to New York City, where I was born and raised." He knew he would take a pay cut, but had no idea how tough it would be. Soon, he realized what a huge gap there was between a green manager and an experienced waiter or bartender.

Reflecting on that time, he notes, "I was the poor guy. I think the biggest part of "the Plan" was getting through that time, always keeping in mind my ultimate goal. With that mind-set, I had put myself in position to let opportunities present themselves. And they did."

Garvey enjoys the challenge of "the unending horizon. There are so many facets within the industry that I enjoy and look forward to experiencing. Then there is the opportunity to get ahead and make money for all of the hard work." He also appreciates the dynamic nature of the business. He notes, "Preparation is critical. Executing the game plan and being able to adjust on the fly is a high."

As far as advice for newcomers to the industry, Garvey shares this tidbit, "I would like to see the work ethic and service aspect of the business go retro. More and more I see a sense of entitlement from people in the industry: 'I just put food in front of you. You owe me 20 percent.' Waitering, as an art form, needs to stage a comeback." He recommends that would-be restaurateurs spend time learning the business, and adds, "Prepare yourself mentally. Although most aspects of the restaurant business are rewarding, don't expect immediate gratification. Like most other businesses, there is a time for paying your dues."

■ ■ ■

"Tell me a little about yourself." It sounds like a pretty simple question. But you'd be surprised how tough it is for some people to answer. The easiest way to keep you from stumbling over this question in an interview situation is to think about it ahead of time—*and* write it down. You don't ever have to show it to anyone. Just get your thoughts together, jot them down, and look for gaps.

But there's a bigger picture reason to do it. Way before the interview, take time to figure out who you are, where you're going, what you *want* from a job, and what you *need* from a job. Answering those questions for yourself is essential *before* you even apply for a job, much less interview for one. This chapter is here to help. Basically, I help you figure out how you like to work and let you decide if the restaurant business might be a good fit for you.

What Kind of Person Are You?

Successful careers in the restaurant business come in all shapes and sizes. But most successful people have a few things in common. Here are a few great traits that can help you succeed in the restaurant business.

- *Upbeat and positive personality.* You don't have to be a sickeningly sweet people person to do very well in this business. But you should be approachable, friendly, and well, nice, at least on the surface. (It's much easier if you are naturally a fairly nice person to begin with, but it's possible to fake it.) When you're working in the front of the house (FOH), basically anywhere the guests can see you, you are on stage, so to speak. Guests should feel comfortable talking to you about their needs, the weather, the décor in the restaurant, or just about anything else. When you're working in the BOH (back of the house, the kitchen store rooms, and so on), you're not on stage, but keeping a positive outlook is helpful in getting extra experience and training that can keep you moving up the ranks in the business. In either situation, you want people to want to be around you.

- *Lots of energy.* The restaurant business is physically demanding, especially when you are first starting out. Early on, you do much of the physical labor and grunt work, like refilling ice wells, carrying boxes of frozen chicken, and cleaning everything from the insides of salt and pepper shakers to the shelves in the dry storage area, with an occasional grease trap thrown in for good measure. And the hours are typically long. New managers often work 70-plus hours per week on a regular basis, sometimes going weeks without a day off. Most of those hours are spent on your feet. You need a good supply of natural energy to keep up and excel in the business.

- *Willingness to learn.* You'll probably start your training by learning the menu items in your restaurant. Don't just stop with the names of the food. Find out what's in each dish, what it tastes like, and how it's prepared. If your restaurant doesn't have a formal training process that requires you to know all the food, learn it anyway. Spend your employee food discounts trying out new items if you have to. Exceed your manager's expectations by learning on your own, and you will soon be out of training and on your way to becoming a senior member of the staff.

- *Curiosity.* If you see something (a dish, a process, a preparation method) that looks interesting, ask about it. Most people who work in restaurants are more than willing to explain what they're doing if you have a genuine interest. (Of course, use your best judgment about the timing of questions; 8:00 P.M. Friday night is probably not a good time to ask the chef about what specials he's whipping up for the following week. He might get a little cranky.) Just don't be afraid to ask questions.

- *Effective listener.* When you get answers to your questions, listen and remember them. Take notes to reinforce what people tell you, and follow up if there's something you don't understand. But if you're the kind of person who needs to have the same information presented multiple times, consider an alternate career. The restaurant industry is too fast paced to hold your hand if you're not making a serious effort to "get it."

- *Ability to take constructive (and not-so-constructive) criticism.*
  Every new restaurant employee makes mistakes, usually
  lots of them. To be successful, you need to learn from
  them quickly, and move on. I wish that every manager
  delivered feedback in a positive and instructive way,
  but that's simply not the way it works. Chefs, in particular, are notorious for being downright condescending
  and belittling employees from time to time. By no
  means are they all like that, but in general, it's more
  truth than legend. When you work in a restaurant, be
  prepared for feedback to be delivered to you in a less-
  than-helpful, sometimes unprofessional way. It's part of
  the culture that's slowly changing. Take it in stride and
  never take it personally.
- *Limited number of visible body modifications.* No matter
  what your personal point of view on piercings, tattoos,
  scarification, and other body modifications, the general
  restaurant-going public doesn't like them. So, many
  restaurants (large and small) have policies in place that
  limit how many and what kind of visible modifications
  their employees may have. Other restaurants have no
  limits of any kind. When you're considering where to
  apply, check out the staff members at your future
  restaurant, and see how your physical appearance com-
  pares to theirs.
- *Genuine interest in the restaurant industry as a career.* As the
  rest of this book shows, the restaurant business if full of

opportunities for learning and making a great life for yourself. If you're a math whiz, learning how to buy products and price a menu to meet your operating costs and make a profit might be the perfect challenge for you. If you like talking to people and getting to know all kinds characters, try your hand at being a bartender or server. And if watching the TV chefs whip up beautiful creations from the most basic ingredients fascinates you, you could be a natural in the kitchen. Think about your long-term potential in the industry, and you're on your way to success.

How Do You Like to Spend Your Day?

Think about how you spend your time. What do you like? What do you wish were different? Do you like or need breaks in your day to squeeze in some meditation? Do you wish you could get away from your current nine-to-five grind? Here are a few different scenarios that may help you decide.

If you're a student trying to schedule your work around a crazy course load, the restaurant business can be a good choice. Many restaurants are closed certain days (sometimes Sunday and/or Monday), which can help free you up for study time and classes. Plus, because many restaurants operate in shifts that correspond with dining periods, like breakfast, lunch and dinner, you may have quite a bit of flexibility in your schedule.

Maybe you have an office job with traditional hours, but you want to augment your income. Consider getting a job working nights or weekends to meet people, work in a fun environment, and earn extra money.

If you have a family with small kids, but you'd like to limit the amount of time the kids are in day care, one parent could get a restaurant job while the other works traditional hours. As one parent gets home from work, the other parent is ready to start the workday. In some cases, parents' work schedules may overlap a few hours on certain days, so they can use part-time child-care.

Actors, dancers, and other entertainers who audition during the weekdays can benefit from having a full-time job during nights, weekends, and holidays. Check out Chapter 5 for information on the work environment to see if it corresponds with how you like to spend your time.

Your Qualities and Qualifications

Think about your entire skill set, not just your restaurant specific experience. (In many cases, you may not have any restaurant experience yet.) Here are a few ideas to get you started.

- Have you had previous success in another industry? Think about past jobs and skills that were important to your success. Are you a great organizer? Are you extremely detail-oriented? Do you have excellent follow-through on projects? Do you work independently?

Do you have experience managing people? All of these skills can benefit you in the restaurant business.

- What kind of customer interaction have you had? Did you work in human resources? Have you had experience in a customer service capacity? Do you have any sales experience? Any of these experiences can help you succeed in the restaurant business.

- If you don't have previous business experience, think about your extracurricular activities in either college or high school. Were you the captain of a sports team, or the president of a club or student organization? That sort of experience shows leadership skills, the ability to stick with something over a period of time, and commitment to making sure a group is running smoothly. All of those qualities are important to being successful in the restaurant business.

- What kinds of volunteer work do you participate in? Volunteerism shows that you have passion about something, whatever it is. So when you're looking for a job-think about any scouting activities, religious organizations, or work at the homeless shelter. If you enjoy working with people, the restaurant business may be right up your alley.

- Do you have interests outside of your work? Do you play guitar in a band or develop web sites in you spare time? Or perhaps you're really interested in cars or crafts. Maybe you never miss the daily news or the

Sunday morning political pundits. Whatever it is, it helps to be well rounded. If you're working in the FOH with customers everyday, being able to discuss a variety of topics and contribute to many different conversations is a plus.

- What kind of people skills do you have? Think about how much customer interaction you like. While it's everyone's job in the restaurant to make guests happy, not everyone enjoys interacting with them. If you can endure people complaining with a smile and a thick skin, you're probably well suited to work with them. If you can't stand the thought of smiling at someone as they send back cold soup, you might want to stick with a kitchen position.

- Are you interested in a job or a career? Even if you have no experience in the business, a career-focused interest could be your ticket to that first job. Restaurant managers spend a ton of time hiring and training new staff members. If you want a career in the business, rather than a new place to collect a paycheck, you have a leg up on the competition because the manager will see you're planning on being around for a while.

Are You a Generalist or a Specialist?

The restaurant business has plenty of opportunities for people who are generalists or specialists, in both the FOH and BOH. And remember, the ultimate generalist in the restaurant is the general manager, hence the title. This person is ultimately responsible for everything in the restaurant from service to sanitation, from hiring employees to purchasing paper goods. She needs to know a little bit (or a lot) about everything that goes on. But you don't need to be a generalist to start out. In fact, most restaurant employees start out specializing in one area.

For example, bartenders are specialists in the FOH, focused on beverages. They make drinks, pour beer, and recommend wines. Some fine dining restaurants have wine specialists called *sommeliers* (pronounced sum-el-YAY) who focus only on the wine lists. Waiters are FOH generalists because they need to know all the food ingredients, preparation methods, points of service, beverage choices, and how to make guests happy.

BOH specialists include line cooks who run a particular station, like the grill. The grill cook may only know how to cook grilled foods and have no knowledge (or even the inclination to know) how to make salads or desserts. The BOH generalists, like the chef or kitchen manager, will (or should) know how to run every station in the restaurant, make every dish, and ensure that everyone is working together properly.

Once you get experience in a particular area, you're likely to become interested in another related area and begin to learn skills and duties of other employees. Before you know it, you'll become a well-rounded restaurant jack-of-all-trades!

Do You Seek Ongoing Challenges?

You'll find no shortage of challenges in the restaurant business. Whether you're just starting your food training or learning how to pair exotic foods with Chilean wines, you'll find plenty of opportunities to learn new things each and every day. It's definitely not boring. Yes, of course, everyone has downtime in the business, but often they're the welcomed lulls that follow periods of crazy-busy shifts.

Because you work with people, you will be challenged to solve problems, anticipate needs, and improve systems, service, and the guest experience. Constantly. No two guests are alike, and you as a restaurant employee, no matter where you work in the restaurant, are required to cater to the guests. It's not always an easy job, I can assure you. It's one of the few constants in the business; you must exceed a guest's expectations if you expect him to come back. And that usually means handling all the challenges with a smile and an outwardly calm appearance.

Do You Prefer to Lead or Follow?

The restaurant business provides excellent opportunities for both leaders and followers. Even if you don't feel like you're management material early on, you might find that you like helping new employees learn the ropes. The next thing you know, you're a trainer in charge of helping new servers learn their food or memorize their table numbers. Or maybe you start out seating people as they come in and eventually work your way up to managing the reservation system.

On the other hand, if you want a career that allows you to come in and do your job, then go home and not take it with you, the restaurant business may be for you. For most employees, you work when you're at the restaurant, and that's it. You leave the stress at the door when you punch out. Owners and managers are, of course, the exception.

Is Money of Prime Importance?

Money is a huge driver for many people. Many of those people are in the restaurant business. But the fact is, very few (seriously, very few) make lots of money. Most who do already had lots to begin with, so they were able to wait out the long, lean years before hitting it big. Or they make incremental income by also cooking on TV, consulting, or selling cookbooks or branded retail products.

In many ways, restaurants are entertainment and relaxation. People in almost all socioeconomic groups frequent restaurants of some sort, and it's not because they all don't know how to cook. In most cases, they come to restaurants to relax, reduce the stress in their days, and just let someone else take over for a while. Your job is to make their experience the best you can. Taking care of their needs, anticipating their wants, and exceeding their expectations is your real job. In short, if you help them feel good, they'll come back again.

If big money is your business, you probably want to find a business other than a restaurant, especially if you think owning your own place is the ticket to riches. If you're happy with a decent wage (on average $25,000 to $60,000 a year depending on where you are in the organization and where you live in the country) in a busy, dynamic environment, by all means read on. It's definitely possible to make $100,000 per year or more, if you're willing to put in your time (many years), think long term, and truly manage your career.

Check out Chapter 4 for details on what positions are available in the industry, and job descriptions and salary information. And don't miss Chapter 9 for tips on managing your career and getting ahead.

What Hours Do You Prefer?

Almost all scenarios are possible in the restaurant business. To be completely honest, though, the nine-to-five scenario is less common. Still, it's definitely possible if you're interested in working in some hotel restaurants or in a restaurant with limited dining periods (perhaps a tea room that's open for lunch only). As an employee rather than an owner, you may be able to work out a regular nine-to-five kind of day. If a nine-to-five schedule is essential to you, give some serious thought to contracted food service, which is basically employee dining facilities and student dining venues at colleges and universities.

In most standard restaurant situations, though, you're likely looking at shift work designed around dining periods—breakfast, lunch, and dinner. Depending on whether you work in the kitchen or the dining room, you'll work for a few hours on either side of the dining period to set up or clean up after it.

Training, Education,
and Background

PROFILE
Pete Mervis
Assistant Manager, Granary
Restaurant at Spring Creek Ranch

Pete Mervis is the assistant manager at the
Granary Restaurant at Spring Creek Ranch in
Jackson, Wyoming (www.springcreekranch.com). A recent graduate of the Hotel and Restaurant Management program at the
University of Denver (DU), this resort restaurant is Pete's first stop
out of school. The restaurant caters to a mix of tourists out to
catch the spectacular view of the Tetons, locals looking for a night

---

out, and hotel guests. The restaurant serves breakfast, lunch, and dinner.

Through a career fair at DU, Pete met a recruiter, which eventually led to an internship and then a permanent position at Spring Creek three and a half months later. Pete's family has roots in the business. His mother runs a catering and spice company in Colorado Springs. His father is a wine consultant.

I asked Pete if they encouraged him to pursue some facet of the restaurant business. Laughing, he said, "If anything, they were almost discouraging. They were supportive, but said, 'Are you crazy? Haven't you seen how hard we work?'" Ultimately, the business is what Pete expected. He knew he'd work long hours, weekends, and holidays.

For the most part, he's only been surprised by nuances of the business. He says, "Communication is such an important thing. I didn't realize how quickly things could fall apart if you're not communicating. We communicate about what we need to do to get a job done, what we can learn from our mistakes, and what not to do again. If you forget to tell someone about an order, it can really mess a lot of things."

Many aspects of the restaurant are appealing to Pete. Trying to work out kinks in a well-established business has been a huge source of creativity for him. He's had to really examine at the best way to get tasks done, looking both at efficiency and ease of compliance. He's hoping that customers will see a change in the service standards at the restaurant in the months to come. Pete also recognizes that every day in the restaurant business is different. He has new diners who haven't been in before, looking to have a fantastic meal in a fantastic setting. Trying to please all those diners at the same time is a challenge that keeps him coming back every day.

Pete has high praise for his educational experience. Earning a Bachelor of Science in business administration, with an emphasis on hotel and restaurant management, provided him with great hands-on experience. He took classes in finance, accounting, and human resources, among other things. Thanks to his coursework, when he looks at his numbers, he knows what he's looking at. He understands why they maybe fluctuating and what he can do to fix a problem. He had many realistic practices and projects. For his final project, he created a restaurant from scratch, doing everything: deciding on the architecture, running the financials, determining the inventory, and creating a purchasing program. He had access to experts in the industry giving talks on how they've gotten to where they are. He's taken advantage of his school's career counselors. "They were very personable. They knew who I was and what I wanted to do. I wouldn't have this job without them."

Pete expects the restaurant business to continue growing in the future. He sees lots of opportunity with his current restaurant and in the business in general. Pete shares some advice with people thinking about pursuing a career like his, "It's a tough business. You're dealing with all different types of people. You really have to understand how people work. You can almost just sense it when they walk in. Eventually, you learn [to anticipate] your guests' needs so you can plan for it." And he urges people to remember that the business is entertainment, saying, "Have fun and challenge yourself, if you're grunting about getting in [to work] maybe it's not for you. It's a great thing, but it has its downsides. If you're not excited to get in, get the work done, and experience new challenges, maybe it's not for you."

When I asked him about his own future in the business, he is hopeful. He definitely looks at this job, and the industry in general, as a great preparation for anything else he may decide to do in the future. He says, " If I leave [the restaurant business], this experience can only benefit me, possibly more than any other industry, no matter what I do in the future."

■ ■ ■

The last 20 years have seen a shift in the industry away from on-the-job training (OJT) and toward industry-related degrees. For the most part, you aren't going to get a job in a restaurant by walking down the street and noticing a Help Wanted sign in the window. (It does happen, but it's the exception these days.)

In this chapter, I talk about the different kinds of training programs available to the would-be restaurant career professional. These days, people looking to make the restaurant business a career get a related degree. Those who don't are often considered temporary, or at least not long-term, employees. New culinarians can pursue an education with a top chef or an apprenticeship program, rather than going to cooking school and still be taken seriously. In fact, many recruiters are like Karen Fox, president of The Hunter Group (www.thehuntergroup.net), a hospitality executive recruiting firm, who says that when she sees a candidate's resume and sees that he's worked for years under a top-notch chef, she knows he has the skills to succeed even if he didn't attend a formal culinary school. She adds, "If they didn't go to school *and* they didn't get hands-on experience from a name chef, it gets a little tougher for them."

Educational and Training Requirements

The restaurant business doesn't require specific degrees, training programs, licensing, or standard examinations like many professions. On a state-by-state basis, restaurant employees may need a few certifications. These certifications are limited to public health and safety concerns rather than any kind of aptitude for the business. Check with your local health department for information on what certifications might be required in your area. Here are a few of the common ones:

- *Food handler card.* Some states require this certification to indicate that the holder has completed a basic food safety test and tested negative for communicable diseases such as Hepatitis-C or tuberculosis. In many cases, all restaurant employees, both FOH and BOH, must have this card on file in the manager's office.

- *Alcohol service certification.* Your state may require that you complete an alcohol service class before you're allowed to serve alcohol to guests. These classes usually cover the alcohol laws of your area, provide information on how to serve alcohol safely, and outline your legal liabilities involved in serving alcohol. A few nationwide alcohol safety training programs, such as Training for Intervention Procedures (TIPS) and ServSafe Alcohol, are available in most areas. Check out www.gettips.com and www.nraef.org respectively for information about classes in your area.

- *Food safety and sanitation certification.* Many states require BOH employees to complete some type of food safety training. The training typically covers information on proper storage of food, safe food rotation, safe thawing procedures, and cleaning and sanitizing work areas. Many restaurants have their own training programs based on their particular facilities, foods, and cleaning products. The government-mandated training is more general and covers material that applies to all restaurants and food service operations. A few national programs exist, including ServSafe (www.nraef.org) and Hazard Analysis and Critical Control Point (HACCP) food safety training at www.cfsan.fda.gov/~lrd/haccp.html.

How Far Can You Go with Various Levels of Training?

You can get started in the restaurant business today without any training or degree. In fact, many people start in this business for that very reason. They can make decent money now rather than waiting to finish a degree. Or they start in the restaurant business temporarily while they're pursuing a degree in a related field or in another area altogether. However, the availability of degree programs has exploded in the last 15 to 20 years, making them accessible to more people in more communities at more universities and other facilities than ever before.

Industry-Specific Degrees

You can find as many names for restaurant-related degrees as you can find schools. Some are four-year programs (usually a Bachelor of Science degree); some are two-year programs (typically an Associate of Applied Science degree). Certificate programs are 18 months, although you can find specialized programs, in pastry, for example, in the 9- to 15-month range as well. Many schools offer apprenticeship programs, co-ops, and externships that may coincide with course work, but they often lengthen the time it takes to get a degree, which needs to be considered in your planning. The upside to those programs is that when you're done, you have academic experience *and* practical experience, theoretically making you more marketable.

Industry-Related Degrees

There are many industry-related degrees. Indeed, there are so many that the list here is not complete. It's intended to give an idea of the range of degrees available. Do your research with the particular schools you're interested in to find out what they offer, the length of the programs, and what kind of job placement assistance they give you when you've completed their programs.

- *Culinary management.* A culinary management degree typically gives you a combination of culinary education with an emphasis on managing people and business processes.
- *Hospitality management.* This degree program generally focuses on business courses (like accounting and economics) with an emphasis on using those skills in a restaurant. Many programs include a class in understanding

the law as it relates to the industry and may have many electives that allow you to focus your coursework on subjects that interest you. You can take classes in golf course design or amusement technology. Sometimes this degree is called an hospitality, restaurant, and tourism management (HRTM) degree or Hospitality and Restaurant Administration (HRA) degree.

Other Helpful Degrees

An accounting degree can be helpful in the restaurant business, just as it can in any business. If you're familiar with profit and loss (P&L) reports, profit margins, and accruals, you'll be that much further ahead in the restaurant business.

A Master of Business Administration (MBA), can be extremely helpful if you're interested in pursuing upper level management and director positions with a restaurant or hospitality company. MBA coursework involves looking at all facets of a business, solving problems, developing new products and markets for existing products, managing people, and a host of other business applications. Few schools (Cal Poly–Pomona and Florida International University) currently offer restaurant- or hospitality-specific MBA programs, but the degree can still offer you some significant advantages.

Some schools, like San Francisco State, offer another type of Master's degree, the Master of Science Business Administration (MSBA). It's designed to allow a student to have more flexibility in developing a personalized curriculum, with an emphasis toward the parts of the hospitality industry that interest them most. Look for more programs like this in the future.

Where Do You Get the Training?

Again, there aren't many requirements in the industry, but the more you know, the more valuable you are to your current and future employer. Continue to invest in your career by keeping up with what's going on in the world of food. Fortunately for you, there is no shortage of training opportunities. Thanks to the nationwide interest in food, cooking, and entertainment, classes are available nationwide that can keep people in the know on where food and restaurants are headed. To find training in your area, try the following suggestions.

Restaurant Associations

Join professional organizations, like the National Restaurant Association (http://restaurant.org/) or American Culinary Federation (www.acf.org). These organizations often host events of interest. Even if you can't attend in person, you might find a transcript online or have an opportunity to order one. Take a look at the appendix for more information on helpful organizations.

Online Sources

More culinary schools and universities are offering online courses so that budding restaurateurs can pursue part of their education at times and places convenient to them. Many online courses are basic sanitation or hospitality courses. Ultimately though, in order to be a well-rounded restaurant professional, you'll need to spend some serious time in a real live restaurant. I recommend online sources for supplemental study and to find out about real hands-on opportunities.

Culinary Schools

So many schools, so little time. Culinary schools offer continuing education programs, certificates, and two- and four-year degrees. They offer a combination of classroom training and extensive hands-on work in kitchens. In some schools, you'll get your practical training in a simulated environment; in others, you'll train in a real working kitchen. The curriculum, coursework, and practical experiences vary greatly, so do some research to see what kinds of programs might fit your goals, schedule, and budget. Make a pit stop in Appendix B to get started.

TOP SCHOOLS FOR DEGREES

Culinary Institute of America (CIA) is recognized as one of the premier culinary programs in the world. It boasts two state-of-the-art campuses, one in Hyde Park, New York, and a second, Greystone, in California's Napa Valley that focuses on continuing education studies. It offers an

Associate degree, a Bachelor of Professional Studies (BPS) that goes well beyond cooking and covers the critical thinking, finance and accounting skills, and technological proficiencies necessary to be a culinary professional, and many certificate programs. Many top-rated chefs attend continuing education classes (www.ciaprochef.com) on a regular basis. Take a look at its web site, www.culilnary.edu, for more information, or contact the program via snail mail at Admissions Department, 1946 Campus Drive, Hyde Park, NY 12538-1499, (800) CULINARY or (845) 452-9430, e-mail: admissions@culinary.edu.

Cornell University School of Hotel Administration offers programs at every level, including degrees, certificates, and continuing education programs for every restaurant employee through its Executive Education program. Many in the industry consider its Masters in Management in Hospitality (MMH) to be *the* graduate degree in the field. This program, started in 1922, was the first hospitality program in the country and is still considered one of the best. You get hands-on training at the Statler Hotel, located on campus and run by the school. You can also take advantage of its online courses. Contact the school at www.hotelschool.cornell.edu or by mail at Cornell University, School of Hotel Administration, Statler Hall, Ithaca, NY 14853, (607) 255-8702 or fax at (607) 255-9243.

University of Nevada–Las Vegas, The William F. Harrah College of Hotel Administration offers a top-notch hospitality program. At the undergraduate level, it offers several restaurant-related degrees, including Bachelor of Science in Hotel Administration and Bachelor of Science in Culinary Arts Management. If you're looking for industry-related graduate coursework, it offers several, including an Master of Hospitality Administration (MHA), an MBA, and a Ph.D. in Hospitality Administration for those interested in research and teaching opportunities. Find out more at http://hotel.unlv.edu or at University of Nevada—Las Vegas, 4505 Maryland Parkway, Box 456013, Las Vegas, NV 89154-6013, (702) 895-3161 or fax at (702) 895-4109.

New England Culinary Institute or NECI (pronounced Neck-ee), graduated TV mad food scientist Alton Brown from *Good Eats* on the Food Network. It offers concentrations in culinary arts, baking and pastry, and management. NECI won the International Association of Culinary Professionals (IACP) award in 2004 for Outstanding Vocation Cooking School. The IACP cited the intensity of its program, which requires 113 credit hours for an AOS degree compared to the more usual 70 or 80 hours. Students acquire real world experience in 11 different food service venues.

Johnson & Wales University has four campuses (Providence, RI; Denver, CO; Charlotte, NC; and North Miami, FL) and two different colleges offering related degrees. The Hospitality College focuses on management degrees (Associate, Bachelor, and certificate programs) whereas the College of Culinary Arts focuses on cooking skills, with concentrations available in food marketing, nutrition, and food service entrepreneurship. Take a look at its web site (http://culinary.jwu.edu) for more information, or contact at Johnson & Wales University, 8 Abbott Park Place, Providence, RI 02903, phone (401) 598-1130.

Universities

Many universities have hospitality schools. Look for schools or colleges within a university with names like "Hospitality," "Hotel," and "Culinary" in the title. Most offer two- and four-year degree programs. The Appendix lists the names of several universities that might have a program for you, and check out Top Schools for Degrees for details on the current best of the best.

Trade Schools and Art Institutes

Many trade, vocational, and technical schools and colleges have culinary programs. Look for DeVry Institute for programs across the country. Many art institutes have culinary programs, because they focus on applied arts. Some also have hospitality programs.

High School Vocational Programs

Large high schools often offer training in the restaurant business through their vocational departments. Some schools have an on-site restaurant run by students that operates during the week at very specific times, usually for lunch. These programs are an excellent way to get hands-on experience in the business without forking out tons of tuition money. One nationwide program founded by the National Restaurant Association's Education Foundation, ProStart, is garnering quite a bit of industry attention.

ProStart (www.nraef.org/prostart) is a two-year training program open to high school students interested in pursuing a career in the restaurant business. Schools pair with industry professionals to give students practical experience in real working restaurants and background information in the classroom. Coursework focuses on all aspects of the restaurant business, from sanitation to safety, nutrition to business math, service standards, and accounting practices. Through the ProStart training program, students can earn a Certificate of Achievement that tells potential employers that they have specific experience in the restaurant business. Students also can earn money as they pursue their certificates. Successful certificate holders are eligible to earn scholarship to pursue additional hospitality and culinary degrees and can earn college credits. Often graduates immediately receive higher pay rate because they have additional, verifiable skills.

On-the-Job Training (OJT)

Ultimately, the choice of whether or not to pursue an industry-related degree is a completely personal one, but it is entirely possible to have a successful career in the restaurant business by pursuing OJT as your primary culinary or food service education. In fact, OJT is usually required. It ranges from a few shifts to months or more. At a minimum, you'll need to get a feel for the internal processes and procedures of a new restaurant. Depending on your experience level, you may need more general training as well.

Apprenticeship Programs

An apprentice works in a real restaurant kitchen under an executive chef with the expectation that the chef will train the apprentice in the culinary arts. Apprenticeship programs are popular for many reasons. On the upside, they tend to be more cost effective than non-apprentice degree programs. You spend less time in a classroom and more time in a restaurant, so you pay less money for your coursework. Often, you also get paid (it's paltry, but it's something) for the hours you work. On the downside, it can take more time (in the neighborhood of three years) to complete an apprenticeship program vs. a degree program of 18 months to 4 years.

Whichever way you go, I recommend that you choose a program that has a great deal of hands-on time in a real restaurant. You need to feel the pressure of a kitchen melting down during a rush on a Saturday night. You need to see how more things can go wrong when it's slow. You need to see the beauty that is the empty dish pit after a long and painful shift.

You have to experience all of these things before you can truly decide to make this business a career.

Training Programs

Many companies have comprehensive training programs that take weeks, months, or sometimes more than a year to complete. In some cases, employees start at the same level, regardless of previous experience or education, and then work their way up through the ranks to top management jobs. These companies feel that this type of training is essential not only for the long-term success of their businesses but also for their employees. An industry-related degree or certificate, however, could give you a leg up, even in these very strict training situations, because it helps you develop the core competencies and fundamentals to excel.

Continuing Education

Any restaurant professional worth her sea salt pursues continuing education opportunities throughout her career. Whether you're a banquet chef who wants to learn how to carve ice or a bar manager looking to beef up on your knowledge of Scotch, all professionals must continue to learn (in a somewhat formal way) throughout their careers. If they don't, they will be passed by those in greater touch with the current industry.

Pay to work in a restaurant. Once you've amassed some experience, you may need some very specific experience (usually in the kitchen) to round out your skill set, in order to take your career to the next level. Some chefs are taking on experienced students for a very short time, one week to one month at most, and letting them work in their world-class kitchens. You pay for the honor and the privilege, and they let you hang out and absorb the knowledge. They also put you to work, doing things like cleaning snails and dequilling squid, but the experience can give you a glimpse into the hidden world of the culinary elite you might not otherwise get. If you're interested in pursuing this option, check with the specific chef you'd like to work with to see what he offers.

Good Qualities for Success

While no two successful restaurateurs are the same, many share similar qualities. All of them have an internal drive to succeed no matter what challenges present themselves, and most have the ability to think on their feet. In this section, I give you insight into some of the most helpful characteristics for the budding entrepreneur.

Self-Motivation

Whether it's asking questions or taking the initiative to do what needs to be done, self-motivated people are successful in the restaurant business. The day-to-day work can be fast paced, followed quickly by periods of painful slowness. Self-motivated people stay focused anytime and are able to get their work done with minimal intervention from higher ups. In restaurants, you don't want to be the squeaky wheel; you want to be the wheel that is able to follow policies and procedures without the grease.

Good Sense of Humor

A sense of humor is an absolute must. Because the restaurant business is ultimately a form of entertainment, you must always have a smile on your face. It's much easier to smile when you find humor in the world around you. All the hard work and time you will put in to your restaurant career is infinitely more enjoyable when you can find the lighthearted side of the odd situations that will inevitably come your way.

Willingness to Try New Things

The restaurant business is always changing. You must be able to adapt and try new ideas. Whether it's a new wine from an unknown vineyard or a new type of fish you've never tried before, you have to explore the world of dining trends in order to pass that excitement along to your customers. What would make customers try a new dish if their server isn't excited about it? How can you try your hand at fish preparation if you're afraid of touching fish guts? No one has the skills until they learn them. Your willingness to learn is one of your greatest assets to your future success.

Tolerance

When you're in the restaurant business, you have to be accepting of lots of personalities, schedules, and priorities that aren't yours. Whether you're dealing with other employees, managers, or a fickle clientele, you have to develop a thick skin.

What Does It Take to Advance?

One of the best things about the restaurant business is that, for the most part, you can really control your own destiny. You have the ability to succeed simply by working hard and learning the business. In this section, I give you tips on getting ahead.

Hard Work

You will work long weekends in this industry, especially when you're just starting out. Be prepared to pay your dues. You'll be on your feet—a lot. No, seriously, a lot. You'll need to keep moving until the last dish is out of the kitchen, the last table leaves, and the last dish is washed. Get some comfy shoes.

Being a Quick Study

The pace of the restaurant demands that you learn quickly. For the most part, you won't have time to make the same mistake twice. Get the basics down quickly, and build from there. Do extra studying on your own time to jump-start your career.

Working Weekends, Holidays, Birthdays, and Anniversaries

It's true. When other people are having fun, you'll be expected to make the fun happen. Hopefully, you'll also be having fun, but sometimes you will miss important events in your personal life. It's up to you to find the balance between your work and your personal life.

High Expectations of Excellence

No matter what business you're in, expect excellence. Set an example in everything you do. Once you learn how to do something, give it your all. Even if it is just cleaning the grease trap, make it the cleanest grease trap in town. Set a higher expectation for yourself than your supervisor does, and you'll exceed his expectations every time.

Positive Energy

Whenever you're in the restaurant, you have to be "on"—all the time. Restaurants that have a positive vibe are the ones that make it. Positive energy is *the* differentiating factor, as intangible as it is, between the winners and the losers. Show your potential employer your energy from the first minute of the first interview.

Passion

In the business, we call it the sickness, the fever, and to succeed long term, you have to have it. Running a restaurant is a business that eventually chooses you; ultimately you can't choose it. If you don't have passion for the business, you can't sustain, maintain, and overcome the obstacles that crop up. You can't teach it or learn it; you have to feel it. If you don't have the passion, your task of becoming successful will be exponentially harder. You have to connect *everything* to your passion.

Hard Work

Did I already mention that? Yes, I did. But I really can't say it too often.

Jobs in
the Industry

At the time, Chef Schadler wasn't interested in cooking as a profession; it was just what the family did. He wanted to be a mechanical engineer. But after talking with other chefs and industry professionals about the international travel and other exciting options, he decided to go into the culinary arts. Forty-five years later, he still loves it.

He started his culinary career with Rock Resorts in 1968 at Caneel Bay Resort on St. John in the U.S. Virgin Islands. In 1981 he joined the Colonial Williamsburg Foundation at its Mobil 5 Star property, the Williamsburg Inn, where he still remains today. He credits both companies with aiding his tremendous professional growth and defining his business sense by establishing ongoing continuing education programs that allowed him to grow in all facets of the business.

Ultimately, his greatest professional love is developing other people. In 1971, he developed the Rock Resort Culinary Apprenticeship program. The program is affiliated with the American Culinary Federation. Since its beginning, the apprenticeship program has graduated many top-notch, nationally recognized chefs. He's committed to developing people the right way, with respect and professionalism.

Currently, Chef Schadler is the Culinary Director of Colonial Williamsburg Hospitality Group (www.cwf.org), which boasts 12 different dining venues, from the upscale Williamsburg Inn, to small family restaurants, museum cafes, golf club restaurants, and colonial taverns, including Christine Campbell's Tavern, which specializes in great seafood. It was one of George Washington's favorites. His current responsibilities are too numerous to list, but they include hiring and training staff, creating menus, developing team concepts, watching over quality and consistency, and maintaining guest survey contacts and perceptions. He has several unit managers who manage different aspects of the day-to-day operations, with a total of 148 culinarians on staff. The Hospitality Group operates a centralized commissary that uses the most modern equipment to produce high quality soups, sauces, dressings, and other food products. There is also a centralized bake and pastry shop that produces many well-known 18th century baked goods for all of the dining venues.

The diversity of the restaurant business is what drives Chef Schadler to stay in it. He loves the day-to-day changes, new opportunities, and the chance to mentor. The industry is ever evolving, keeping you fresh and sharp, giving you instant rewards. In the fall of 2005, he created a white truffle dinner that coincided with a concert by Italian tenor, Andrea Bocelli. Other days he serves heads of state (nearly 60 over his career). But most often he deals with everyday people enjoying a meal in one of his restaurants. "I get to touch people and have an impact on them." For him, each day is something new. He's a learner, always. During his 45 years in the business, he's had to adjust his style and philosophy, rapidly at times. But he still has his fundamental philosophies. Ultimately, he can hold his own with any contemporary today. He's made it a mission to keep learning and keep current in an ever-changing business. "You can't stand still or you won't last long with competition and changes. The 'old way' isn't necessarily the best way anymore."

He credits his wife, Liv, as the biggest support in his career, enabling him to do what it took to become successful. Fortunately, she and their girls are very understanding and always prepared for whatever Hans is into, namely 15 hour work days, six to seven days a week, at many exotic locations in the world. His time at home with the children when they were small was limited but special; he admits that he probably sees them more often now than when they were in school. As he built his career, his responsibilities grew, and ultimately his time commitment to his job grew. "My wife raised the children, I provided for them. My wife is my partner. But there have always been trade-offs." He says he still struggles with the balance between family and career. In a resort environment, his family has an incredibly good lifestyle, traveling to many of the best places, staying in luxurious accommodations.

■　■　■

The front of the house (FOH in written but not spoken restaurant lingo) is the part of the restaurant that the guests or diners see. So the dining room, bar, restrooms, and lobby are all part of the front of the house. The back of the house (BOH) is the part of the restaurant that guests typically don't see. Areas like the kitchen, storerooms, and managers' offices are part of the back of the house. Often, restaurant job seekers start out in one area or the other. Eventually, if you want to be a truly successful restaurateur, you'll need experience in both areas and most positions. The next sections give a quick survey of the different positions in each area of the restaurant, so you can get a feel for how each position works, what the salary expectations are, and how they all work together to make a restaurant successful.

Common Entry-Level Jobs and Salaries

Everybody has to start somewhere, and in the restaurant business, it's no different. Most people start out in one of the common entry-level restaurant jobs in one of the areas of the restaurant. If you have a good attitude, are well groomed, and are on time for your interview, here's where you can get a job today without any experience!

Front of the House Staff

In this section, I describe some of the common entry-level FOH positions. I also include information about what kind of salary you can expect when you're starting out.

Greeter/hostess. Different restaurants have different titles for these positions. Whatever they call them, these people are often the first restaurant employees a guest sees in a casual, family, or fine dining restaurant. (QSR and fast casual restaurants do not typically employee greeters.) Greeters welcome diners to the restaurant, show them to their tables, and provide menus. They may also answer the phone, take reservations, or take to-go orders, depending on how the restaurant system works. In fine dining establishments, greeters may also pull out chairs for guests and help them place linens in their laps. Greeters may be expected to check and restock restrooms as needed.

Often these employees are either too young to work as servers or bartenders (depending on the liquor laws of a given state), or they are required to serve in this capacity before promotion to another level in the restaurant. You can expect to make an hourly minimum wage up to $9 per hour (depending on your experience level and tenure) and expect to work 20 to 25 hours a week as a greeter. In some restaurants, greeters (along with food runners and bussers) are also paid a portion of tips because they're considered support staff. If you receive tips, you'll typically receive a lower hourly wage.

Cashiers. Cashiers work in casual and QSR restaurants. In QSR, diners place their order with the cashier, pay for their meals, and then wait while they are prepared. In casual restaurants, diners typically pay the cashier after they've eaten, usually on the way out of the restaurant. In some restaurants, greeters serve double duty as cashiers. You can expect to make between minimum wage and up to $7 an hour (depending on your experience level and tenure with a company) and expect to work 20 to 25 hours a week as a cashier.

Bussers. Bussers clear, clean, and reset tables in preparation for the next set of diners. They also may help keep server stations stocked with ice, glassware, silverware, and so on. In some fine dining restaurants, FOH employees are required to spend time as bussers before moving on to waiting tables. In other restaurants, busser positions are filled by employees too young to wait tables or serve alcohol. (The age varies depending on the liquor laws of the state.) Bussers typically make between minimum wage and $7 an hour. Depending on the restaurant, they may also receive a share of tips.

Food runners. Food runners typically work only during busy periods to help waitstaff get food to the table quickly. They focus on running food from the kitchen to the guests when it's ready, so that diners get their food at the right temperature: hot food hot and cold food cold, never lukewarm. When appropriate, food runners may also offer condiments (fresh cracked pepper on salads, parmesan cheese on pasta, or ketchup with fries) to go with the food served. In some cases, food runners are too young to wait tables; in others, waitstaff are required to work food running shifts to learn what each dish looks like, familiarize themselves with the steps of service in the restaurant, and get a feel for how everything works. Food runners typically make minimum wage, plus a portion of tips from the waitstaff.

Back waiter. In many traditional, fine dining establishments, someone who wants to be a professional waiter starts as a back waiter. It's on-the-job-training for the back waiter and support for the current waitstaff all rolled into one. One back waiter may assist a team of waiters with serving bread, refilling glasses, carrying trays, and so on, all the while learning the food on the menu, the steps of service in the restaurant, and the basic processes around the restaurant. In most cases, you'll only find back waiters in fine dining establishments. Back waiters typically make minimum wage and may make a portion of pooled tips.

Bar back. A bar back helps a bartender keep the bar stocked during busy shifts. She may wash glasses, stock ice, keep coffee going for warm drinks, and restock beer. She's the extra set of hands on busy nights. In some restaurants, bartenders take turns serving in this role; in others, bartenders start as bar backs and work up to bartenders. Expect to make minimum wage, plus a portion of pooled tips.

Back of the House Staff

Here's a collection of job description for common entry level BOH jobs available in most restaurants. I describe the typical responsibilities for each position and give you salary information, so you'll know what to expect.

Dishwashers. The dishwasher may seem like a lowly position in the restaurant, but no restaurant can be successful without one. These people are some of the hardest working people in the restaurant. It's a place to start in the business if you have no experience but have an interest in the business. Some restaurants require all kitchen staff to start here before they can ever touch a stove and work their way up. In addition to washing dishes, dishwashers are often responsible for taking out the trash and washing the floors at night. You can expect to make between minimum wage and $8 an hour as a dishwasher depending on the cost of living in your area. In urban areas, you may make closer to $10 to $12.

Prep cooks. This position is the entry level cooking position in any restaurant. Typically, these cooks work nonpeak hours and "prep" (or prepare) many of the parts of menu items ahead of time. Because many items in a restaurant are made from scratch and the recipe may have many steps, restaurants typically plan out the parts of the dish that they can prepare ahead of time. For example, in an Italian restaurant, prep cooks make the pasta in large batches. In a Chinese restaurant, they likely trim the snow peas and other vegetables to get them ready for various stir-fries. And in a seafood restaurant, they may peel and devein the shrimp. Some restaurants keep a prep cook on hand during busy times as well to keep the kitchen stocked as the line cooks prepare the shift's meals to order. You can expect to make between minimum wage and $10 an hour as a prep cook.

Pantry cook. A pantry cook position is usually the entry level line cook position in a restaurant. In most cases, a pantry cook isn't cooking at all. He's assembling cold foods (like salads), cold appetizers (like shrimp cocktail), and desserts. This person has to be able to work quickly and efficiently as orders come in, but he doesn't usually need the expertise to create menu items from scratch to order. You can expect to make between $6.50 and $9 as a pantry cook.

Crew/team member. This is the term that QSR restaurants use for their nonmanagement positions. Whether you work drive-through, cashier, or cook, you're probably called a team member. Expect to make around $7 to $9, maybe 50 percent more in urban areas.

A Likely Career Path

One of the best things about the restaurant business is that in many ways you control your own destiny. People with a wide range of education and experience levels have made huge and quick strides in the business. There's no set time for "paying your dues." Some people that have a real knack for the business can skyrocket from busboy to GM of a casual restaurant within seven to ten years, and others with an industry degree cut out many of the traditional steps along the way. But, as an illustration, here are a few typical (if there are such things) career paths in the business:

1. FOH career plan: greeter → busser → back waiter → waiter → head waiter/trainer → assistant manager → general manager.

2. BOH career plan: dishwasher → prep cook → pantry cook→ line cook → sauté cook → sous chef → executive sous chef → executive chef.

Mid-Level Jobs and Salaries

The mid-level jobs in restaurants are a wide category. They include both experienced employees and managers at many different levels, in both the FOH and BOH. As a result, you see a wide range of salaries in the business. Also, there's a section here for trainers.

Front of the House Mid-Level Positions

This section highlights jobs in the FOH that you might qualify for if you've been in the restaurant business for a bit. Each position includes information about required experience and salary information.

Bartenders. In a nutshell, bartenders pour drinks. Depending on the restaurant and the steps of service, atmosphere, and so on, bartenders may have other responsibilities as well. In some cases, diners can experience the full menu in the bar. Some restaurants require bartenders to be as experienced with the food menu as they are with the bar menu. In others, if a patron chooses to eat at the bar, a food server will attend to her. Because the bar requires efficiency, speed, and a strong working knowledge of beers, wines, and spirits, most restaurants require bartenders to have experience before hiring them, sort of a catch-22 for the entry level bartender. Some waiters move over to the bar once they've mastered the food of the restaurant. In other cases, bartenders start as bar backs. Still others attend a short-term bartending class that offers help with job placement.

Bartenders usually make minimum wage, plus tips from bar patrons. If the bar is part of a restaurant, the bartender usually is "tipped out" by the waitstaff, meaning the waiters and waitresses tip the bartender a portion of their earnings for the shift, usually equivalent to between 8 to 15 percent of the server's alcohol sales for the shift. A good bartender can take home anywhere from $40,000 to $80,000 a year, depending on where he works.

Waitstaff. Some restaurants call them servers, waiters, waitresses, guest service experts, service team members, or even sales associates. Whatever you call them, these people have the primary direct contact with the guests. They explain the menu, make recommendations, bring drinks, take orders, serve food, and provide the guest with anything else they may need while they're in the restaurant. Typical restaurant waiters make an hourly wage, usually half of minimum wage plus tips, which range from 15 to 20 percent of their sales each shift. The more products you sell, the more tips you make, usually. Depending on how much a server works (part time vs. full time) and the price of the food he or she is serving, expect to make between $200 to $800 a week. Some experienced professional waiters working in fine dining establishments make upwards of $60,000 a year or more. (Some private clubs, like country clubs for example, pay servers an hourly rate in the $8 to $12 per an hour range in lieu of tips.)

Captains. The captain system is used in some fine dining restaurants. A waiter with considerable experience, leadership ability, and tenure with the restaurant will act as a leader during and often after a shift to ensure that everything runs smoothly during a shift and the restaurant is properly cleaned and reset at the end of the shift. Depending on the restaurant, a captain may have additional specialized responsibilities, like making tableside desserts or doing wine service. Captains are financially compensated in a variety of ways. They may receive a monthly salary (maybe an additional $400 a month) or a larger share of pooled tips. Or they may be rewarded with more opportunities to make more tips (like larger sections or private parties with guaranteed tips). In most cases they also have a higher hourly rate (somewhere in the neighborhood of $6 to $7 per hour rather than half of minimum wage).

Trainers

Trainers operate in both the FOH and BOH in all restaurants at some level. They may be seasoned employees within a restaurant, or corporately trained teams that move from restaurant to restaurant, ensuring quality and consistency.

Employee trainers. Most restaurants employ trainers to (surprise!) train other employees. Trainers can be found in either the front or back of the house (some do both). They take new employees through the processes of the restaurant, show them the food, teach them the steps of service, and generally show them the ropes. Typically, the trainer receives a higher hourly wage ($5 or $6 an hour) during the shifts they train. They may also receive other perks, like a preferred schedule, sections, or tables and free meals.

Corporate trainers. Corporate casual restaurants employ teams of trainers that come in and open a new restaurant location. They may have minimanager responsibilities, like screening applicants, checking references, and conducting interviews. But their primary role is to train crews of new employees how to work in the restaurant within the corporate standards and systems. Ultimately, they ensure consistency between locations whether they restaurant is located in Boston or Boise. They introduce the culture of the restaurant to the new employees, drill them on menu ingredients and preparation methods, and put them through mock dining situations. In short, they conduct a training boot camp before a new property opens. Once the store is up and running, usually a month or two after opening, corporate trainers move on to another new property.

Back of the House Mid-Level Positions

This section highlights jobs in the BOH that you might qualify for if you've had some experience in the restaurant business.

Line cook. Line cooks run each station in a restaurant. Most restaurants divide the line (the area in the kitchen where food is prepared to order) by preparation method and call those areas *stations*. Examples include the fry station, thc grill, and the sauté station. Different restaurants have different stations depending on their menus. Different stations on the line usually require different levels of expertise (typically sauté is the most intense), and cooks receive a varying pay rate depending on their experience, usually in the $8 to $15 an hour range. In QSR, because most items aren't made from scratch, to order, the pay range is lower for line cooks (or team members) and runs from minimum wage to the $7 an hour range.

Sous chef. A sous chef is the chef's second in command. (*Sous* means "under" in French and is pronounced "soo.") A sous chef's responsibilities vary with each restaurant, but often they have some people management responsibilities, often closing the restaurant and ensuring sanitation schedules are followed, food is put away properly and counted, and the prep list is ready for the following day. Or a sous chef may open the restaurant, receive orders from vendors, and get the day going. A sous chef is a leader in the kitchen, but is also learning from the chef. He can expect to make an hourly wage of $10 to $18 or salary of $25,000 to $40,000 a year.

Expediter. Usually called an *expo* but sometimes called a *quality assurance supervisor* in more casual restaurants, this position is responsible for making sure that food comes out of the kitchen on time, all together (all dishes go to the same party together), at the appropriate temperature, and up to any other restaurant standards. She communicates constantly with all the stations on the line, servers as necessary, and all managers in the restaurant to make sure food and orders flow in and out of the kitchen at the proper pace. Anyone, employee or manager, who needs to communicate with the kitchen (or anyone in the kitchen) during a busy shift communicates through the expo. Depending on the way a restaurant runs, someone may be hired to run this position specifically, or the chef or another manager may perform it. If the expediter is hired specifically to perform this job, he can expect to make $10 to $13 an hour.

Management

Most mid-level managers in restaurants make between $28,000 and $50,000 plus a bonus, depending on experience, geographic location, and type of service. Although they are often in charge of specific areas of a restaurant, they perform the same general sorts of functions.

A few general examples of manager duties are:

- Hiring, training, motivating, and supervising staff members to ensure excellent performance and quality service standards are achieved
- Maintaining proper cost controls
- Scheduling staff members and coordinating food service during shifts
- Maintaining sanitation schedules in their areas
- Working with other managers and employees to ensure complete guest satisfaction

A few specialized mid-level manager titles that you may see on job ads, with a brief description of their specific responsibilities are:

- *Bar manager.* Responsible for purchasing all liquor, wine, spirits, garnishes, and paper goods and for maximizing profits and managing staff in the bar. They come up with the cool drinks menu, interact with beverage

companies, and keep in touch with the bar scenes in their establishments.

- *Kitchen (or culinary) manager (KM).* Some restaurants, often corporate chains, operate without a formal chef and instead hire someone to perform many chef-like functions, like purchasing and controlling costs. The big difference here is that KMs don't typically get involved in menu development. The KM gets the corporate manual of what to order, where to buy it, and how much to pay for it. They get a production manual with recipes on how to make the various dishes the restaurant serves. They are efficient and typically follow directions well. They are assessed by how consistent and within standards the food is, rather than rewarded for innovation, as a chef might be.

- *Dining room manager.* Sometimes called a service manager, this manager is primarily responsible for the front of the house staff and the flow of the dining room during shifts. She likely won't have much purchasing involvement. She may oversee staff training and development and be in charge of maximizing sales through training servers to *upsell* (sell more expensive or additional items that enhance the guest's experience at the restaurant).

- *Banquet manager.* This title is also a hotel title, but can be used in a large restaurant that does quite a bit of banquet or on-premise catering work. A banquet manager works with wedding planners, event planners, and regular people who want to host events at the restaurant. They help people celebrate important events. They work to organize, set up, and run large functions. They manage the logistics of the staff, food, and equipment necessary to complete each event.

- *Catering salesperson.* Depending on where a restaurant does its catering (off site or at its own facility), this person may also be called a special events manager. Ideally, people in this role generate new business for the restaurant through booking, planning, and overseeing large events such as weddings, conferences, and holiday parties. This person communicates extensively with the guest beforehand to ensure the event runs smoothly. In many restaurants, another manager handles this function until the catering end of the business becomes extensive and profitable enough to hire someone to manage this specific business.

Top-Level Jobs and Salaries

In the restaurant business, top-level is in the eye of the beholder. Some people believe you must be a world-renowned chef with your own line of cookware to be top level. Others believe you can start your own place from the ground up, have a loyal clientele, a great reputation, and be a top-level restaurateur. Because we have so many definitions of success in this business, several job descriptions are covered in this section. And at this level of the business, the

FOH and BOH don't often apply, because to reach the top, you have to be well-rounded and have expertise in both areas of the business.

Food and beverage (F&B) manager/director. This title is often used in hotels. Large hotels have many restaurants, but a single F&B manager in charge of purchasing and cost controls for all. An F&B director can expect to make $50,000 to $80,000, possibly more with bonuses.

Executive chef. In a nutshell, the executive chef is responsible for profitability, quality, and innovation in the kitchen. He ensures that the menu matches the concept and the food exceeds guests' expectations. He hires, trains, and schedules the kitchen staff. He establishes and maintains sanitary standards for the kitchen. He negotiates favorable pricing agreements with vendors and orders food as needed. He is ultimately responsible for the food cost percentages for the restaurant. Executive Chefs make anywhere from $35,000 to $150,000 per year; however, most make between $40,000 and $90,000.

Part of the reason for this huge pay range is because the title Executive Chef has become diluted over the last 20 years or so. Many people receive this title in lieu of financial compensation, often well before they've "earned" it according to the more traditional path. Some people have the title after three to five years in the business, especially if they've spent time in smaller venues. Hotels and corporations tend to have fairly strict schedules (a minimum of nine to ten years if you've been to school) for bestowing these titles upon culinarians. More than with any other position in the business, the pay rate is definitely dependent on the facility or property and the chef's experience, accolades, ability to manage others, and reputation in the business, along with a host of other factors.

General manager. In independent restaurants, the general manager (GM) is typically in charge of everyone in the restaurant. The GM may also be the owner of the restaurant. In many corporate environments, the Executive Chef and the GM are equal, and report to someone else up the corporate chain. Ultimately, the GM and the Executive Chef work together to create a successful and profitable restaurant, including hiring and training quality managers. GMs often build the business by being the face of the restaurant in the community. They may join civic organizations in order to build or extend networking opportunities, which ultimately build up the restaurant. Depending on the sales of the restaurant and the location, GMs typically make between $70,000 to $150,000 a year, including bonuses. Their compensation may also include an equity stake in the restaurant.

Corporate Management

While some restaurants are independent, many are part of a chain or restaurant corporation of some kind. Corporate managers perform functions that assist several restaurants at once. In this section, I give you information about some of the specific positions available in corporations at this level.

Multiunit managers. These positions, also known as regional or district managers, are common in chain and corporate restaurants. These managers interact with GMs of individual restaurants within a region or district. If the restaurant is set up as a franchise (see Chapter 10 for more information on franchises), the owner of the franchise may hire a single multiunit manager to oversee all the restaurants he owns. Basically, these managers make sure all the restaurants in the group are run consistently. They look at financial plans, safety records, employee training programs, sanitation systems, health inspection reports, hire managers, and do anything else that's appropriate to their business. In some corporate environments, this position is called director of operations. The salary range for this position is typically $95,000 to $150,000 annually.

Purchasing manager. Many restaurant corporations employ purchasing managers or directors. They oversee company-wide purchasing issues; for example, they negotiate more favorable vendor agreements based on purchasing for all the restaurants at once. They evaluate new products recommended by vendors. They work with the executive chef(s) and GM(s) to conduct product tests of new and alternative products. They manage inventory levels of products used in the restaurants.

The salary range for this position is $50,000 to $85,0000 per year.

Corporate chef. A corporate chef may be in charge of innovation and quality for all the restaurants in the corporation. Often, they spearhead menu changes, limited time offers, and favorable purchasing agreements. They typically work closely with other corporate team members on financial systems, such as food costing and menu pricing. A corporate chef can expect to make between $60,000 and $150,000 a year, plus bonus. The corporate chef may also receive an equity stake in the business or profit sharing.

Other opportunities. Most restaurant corporations employ other standard business positions in areas like marketing, finance, accounting, human resources, and legal affairs. These people operate as they would in any business setting; their business just happens to be restaurants.

CHAPTER 5

The Working
Environment

When Jordan Holcomb was 15 years old, he lived
with his older brother who was a cook in a restaurant in Charleston,
South Carolina. The brothers were scrounging around for a snack
one day and the pickings seemed slim, so Jordan decided on a
frozen pizza. Out of the same fridge, his brother put together a fantastic meal for himself. As Jordan envied his brother's meal, he

made a life changing decision. He wanted to be a chef. He went down to the restaurant where his brother worked the next day and got a job washing dishes.

Jordan bugged the chef nearly every day for six months until he got work in the pantry. Jordan stayed at the restaurant until he graduated from high school, working his way through many of the stations on the line. After graduation, he enrolled at the New England Culinary Institute (NECI) and earned an Associate degree. His career goals were broad: He wanted to be a sous chef by 25 and an executive chef by the time he was 30. He exceeded his own expectations by becoming a sous chef by 22 and an executive chef by 26. Now, he wants to expand on his FOH training and eventually move into a food and beverage director position.

Chef Holcomb hires employees with and without industry-related degrees. He recommends that if you choose to go to school, choose the right school for you. NECI was exactly what he wanted—a one-year degree, with six or seven students per chef. He liked the hands-on experience of working in a real restaurant, not just a classroom, six days a week, 12 hours a day.

Chef Holcomb's biggest surprise after getting into the restaurant business was the different temperaments of people who make up the industry. The first chef he worked for was the more traditional "yeller and screamer." But every experience since then has been surprisingly pleasant.

Currently, Chef Holcomb is the executive chef at the Granary Restaurant at the Spring Creek Ranch in Jackson Hole, Wyoming. His company doesn't give incentives for people with culinary degrees. To get a feel for their talent and abilities, they look at the whole of a potential employee's experience, including school. Chef Holcomb says, "Some of the best cooks I've worked with are from the School of Hard Knocks." He requires all potential employees to work with his staff for two days before offering them permanent positions. Ultimately, he feels he can train just about anyone if he or she is a good fit with the existing team. He's very visible in his restaurant, making passes through the dining room, speaking with guests about their meals and the experience at the Granary.

Two key things keep Chef Holcomb in the business, the challenge of the industry and the flexibility of the lifestyle. "No matter how good you are, there's always room for improvement. I like having a new adventure to solve. If there were no problems in food service, no one would be doing it," he contends. Before he became the executive chef, he liked working nights and having his days free. He's an avid fly fisherman. He used to spend his mornings fishing, then come in to start his night shift between 1 and 3 P.M. He enjoyed staying up late at night interacting with his co-workers when he was starting out.

Now as an executive chef, he has less free time, and virtually no time to hang out with employees socially, but he still loves the business.

If he could change anything in the industry, it would be "the old school mentality. There's just lots of ego and attitude out there." He recommends that people take the time to prove their abilities, instead of just demanding a high starting wage. That's how he hired his sous chef, Ash Tucker, whom he credits with being part of his own success at the restaurant.

For people considering a career in the industry, he recommends trying some jobs before going to school. "Get a job working in kitchens during high school. Make sure you like it before dropping $60,000 on school. Realize that when you sign up to be [in the business] for the rest of your life, holidays and weekends don't exist. It's hot as hell in the kitchen; you're sweating and working fast. It's definitely not a business for people who don't have anything else to do. You gotta' love it."

■ ■ ■

One of the things that draws potential employees to the restaurant business is the fun. They see the excitement of people celebrating special events, like engagements, birthdays, and graduations. They see smiling faces as people are delighted by the new taste sensations. They recognize the party atmosphere of people having a good time. And they decide they want to be part of that. These reasons are all good ones for having an initial interest in the restaurant business. But remember, the reality of the business can tarnish that illusion if you don't go into the business with your eyes and mind wide open. In this chapter, I show you how to develop realistic expectations of what the day-to-day working environment of the restaurant business is like, so you can make an informed decision about how you might fit in.

Lifestyle, Culture, and Attitudes

Every industry has its own personality. In the restaurant business, this personality influences the lifestyle of the people who work in it and the daily work life and pace of the restaurant. In this section, I include information about some of the key elements of the personality of the business.

Work Hard, Play Hard

Restaurant employees work hard. All of them, all the time— during a shift, that is. At all levels of the business, from fast food to the finest dining establishments, from team members to managers, everyone works hard. This hard-core work ethic permeates the industry and binds it together. If you're not working hard, people will notice, and you won't last long.

And don't think it's up to the managers and shift supervisors to let you know if you're not pulling your weight. The restaurant business comes with the ultimate peer pressure. Your co-workers will let you know how you're doing. In this business, no news is good news; you might not hear from them if you're doing a good job. If you're doing an unsatisfactory job, though, you're guaranteed to hear about it. Ultimately, there is no time for slackers in the business. You must pull your own weight; because there's so much work to do, no one wants to do their own *and* yours.

The Ying to the hardworking Yang is that restaurant people play hard, too. They aren't afraid to sample their own wares and celebrate the end of a long (and sometimes painful) shift with co-workers till the wee hours of the morning. Many restaurant employees need to decompress after the pressure of a shift. And frankly, because they work later in the evening than their regular-job peers, they are drawn to each other socially. Long after your office-job friends have gone home and gone to bed, you may still be cleaning grease traps, filling up salt and pepper shakers, or counting food. Who doesn't need to celebrate after that?

Every night it's happy hour somewhere, usually at a bar that stays open later than the restaurant where you work. It's very easy to get drawn into this scene, but heed a word of warning. If you're in management (or plan to go into management), I recommend that you always keep your drinking under control when in the company of fellow employees. Even if you don't drink alcohol, you may find it very easy to become part of the cycle: Working till 11 P.M. or midnight, staying out with friends until 2 or 3 A.M.; sleeping until noon or 1 P.M.; and then starting it all over again. If you have no other responsibilities (family or school, for example), that schedule may be OK for you, at least for a while. But recognize that it's not a schedule that career-focused, upwardly mobile people can really keep up with for very long.

Tolerance

The restaurant business is open to people from all walks of life. That's true across the board, whether it's a restaurant in an urban environment or in the heart of small-town America. Expect to work with Latinos, Africans, Asians, Eastern Europeans, African Americans, and people from the gay and lesbian community. If they work hard, everyone is accepted in the restaurant business.

In some cases, you'll be working with people (especially in the BOH) that don't speak English at all. It's not a requirement. Because so much of restaurant work is physical, a new immigrant can walk into a restaurant (with the appropriate legal paperwork, of course) and get a job making decent money today. They may be learning English while they work in an attempt to eventually work their way up through the ranks of the industry in pursuit of the American dream. Or they may simply be working to send money to their families back home. Either way, the restaurant business is supportive of new immigrants.

People with an alternative lifestyle hold a special place in the restaurant community. Gays and lesbians are accepted without reservation in this industry. They feel comfortable being part of the restaurant community. Most are very open about their lifestyles here, whereas they may not be in, say, a corporate working environment. If you're not comfortable with it, get comfortable with it, or at least accept it. It's a big part of the industry, and it's not going away.

Ethics

As in any industry, there are ethical people and unethical people. Ultimately, you have to be able to trust the people you work with, and they have to trust you. You work side by side with each other and depend on each other during very hectic shifts. If you work in the FOH, you're also working with hundreds (maybe thousands) of dollars per shift and must be able to trust your co-workers. If you feel like you can't trust your supervisors and co-workers, you should probably find another restaurant. Most are run ethically, so it shouldn't be hard to find them.

The Workplace and Work Pace

I like to think of the pace in terms of a sports analogy. You have your pre-game meeting to get all the players psyched up and focused. Then you have the actual game where you execute everything you've planned and practiced for. And finally, you have your post-game period when you let down a little, but analyze everything that went right and wrong. You formulate a plan for making changes and improving performances.

The restaurant business follows a similar cycle. You have your prep time getting ready for guests to arrive. Your guests arrive, and you put on your show. Then after they're gone, you bask in the glow and figure out how to do it even better next time.

Co-Workers

The National Restaurant Association has a profile of the typical foodservice employee:

- Female (55 percent)
- Single (68 percent)
- Working part time and averaging 25 hours a week
- Under 30 years of age (52 percent)
- Living in a household with two or more wage earners (79 percent)

Beyond that, the employee mix is racially diverse and currently includes 19 percent Hispanics, 10 percent African Americans, and 7 percent Asian Americans. You'll also probably have some foreign-born workers.

You'll work with people who are temporary and people who are "lifers." These days, more of the lifers are considered professional, career-oriented people, rather than those who just accidentally wandered into the business. Even if they started out as temporary, they see the opportunity to make a true career doing something they enjoy and are good at. But because the restaurant business is easy to get started in, you may have a constant revolving door of new employees as well as a core group of long-term employees around you.

Try Before
You Buy

part-time job. She continued to work her day job and also worked at Galloway Station on Friday nights and all day Saturday. That was three years ago.

Now Amanda is the server captain at this immensely popular bar and grill in Springfield, Missouri. She trains all the new employees for three or so shifts before they're on their own. Given the relaxed atmosphere at this bar, that's plenty of training. Most of the training focuses on the basics. McDermitt says, "Our training's pretty informal. It's focused on relating with the customers more so than other places. Here, there's less of a barrier between customers and staff. Customers are more like friends than guests. I encourage the staff to sit down with them and talk."

The customers at this open restaurant expect that kind of attention. Located near a popular nature trail, customers walk, bike, and bring their dogs by to drink from the water bowls outside. Amanda teaches the waitresses to greet regulars by name and know their drink orders. Her natural ease with guests is hard for most newbies to replicate, as it comes with experience. And her rapport with kids is amazing. If a child is at the table, Amanda almost always addresses them first. Kids and parents alike appreciate the extra attention.

Despite her increased responsibilities at the restaurant, this job is part time for her. She's a student, pursuing a degree in sign language interpretation. Once she graduates, she's considering blending the restaurant business with her interest in providing resources to the deaf community. She's looking for ways to develop a training program to provide job training and placement services to members of the deaf community.

Even though she hasn't pursued an industry-specific degree, Amanda loves the business and her current restaurant. "When I think about leaving here, it means leaving my friends. I just think about the people I never would have met if I hadn't worked here." Indeed the people are what she loves about the business, "My customers are my audience. I get to tell as many jokes as I want to. If they don't laugh. I leave them alone. Then I can wander around and play with kids." Hers is a humorous understatement, especially if you watch her at work on a weekend night, but it really underscores how much fun the business can be with the right attitude.

I asked Amanda for her advice for those interested in getting into the restaurant business. She had this to say, "Be ready to work. And don't let things bother you. Don't take things personally. Let it all roll off your back. If you get down, it'll show to the customers. Stay up, stay positive all the time." And maybe most importantly she adds, "Enjoy!"

■　■　■

Taking on a new career is scary for anyone. Whether you're completely new to the working world or comfortable in your current career, if you're reading this book, you're probably contemplating making the leap into the restaurant business. This industry is an ideal industry to try out before you take the big step and quit your day job. In this chapter, I give you ideas and concrete tips for pursuing part-time and temporary jobs in the restaurant industry. And I help you find ways to get the most from the experience, helping you get the specific skills you need to move your career into gear. Additionally, I give you information on which skills to gain (and how to get them) before you take the bigger step of starting your very own restaurant.

Part Time May be the Right Time

Nearly 40 percent of all restaurant employees work part time. In some cases, they work at multiple restaurants, part time at each to make up a full-time schedule. In other situations, they work in restaurants because they're trying to schedule their jobs around something else, such as family, school, or auditions, or jobs in different industries. Flexibility is one of the most often cited positives about working in the restaurant industry.

Managers can typically work around all kinds of schedule requirements. Whether it's working around your class schedule or accommodating your daughter's spring dance recital, most restaurants keep enough staff members to allow everyone to have some flexibility. I recommend that if you have specific schedule requirements, discuss those up front with your prospective manager. You need to know what can realistically fit into your life and still meet the restaurant's requirements. For example, some restaurants absolutely refuse to allow time off during the holidays. If you have a standing annual gig as the evening Santa at a major mall, you're probably not a good fit for that particular restaurant. But don't go into to a job interview asking for every Friday and Saturday night off. They'll laugh you right out the front door and drop your application in the circular file (aka, the trash can).

Taking a part-time job in a restaurant is a great way to gain experience. You learn about the pace of the business. You'll see how quickly you pick up the process, the system, and the flow of the restaurant you're working in. You'll figure out how quickly you catch on to learning the menu, the steps of service, and the layout of your new place. And ultimately, you'll figure out how much you like (or loathe) learning it all.

Part time can give you a true taste of the business that no book (no, not even this one) can match. After working a 17-hour brunch shift on Mother's Day, you'll know if the business is for you. Once you miss New Year's Eve with your friends and family in favor of hauling the trash outside and hosing down greasy floor mats, you'll know if you have the passion to make this business your life.

I recommend that you give a restaurant part-time job a full year before you make any permanent decision about the industry and your place in it. That way, you'll get a feel for the ebb and flow of the annual business cycles. You'll get a chance to see how any weather changes in your area affect your business. And chances are, you'll have missed a few important events in your personal life during that time period. Often, how we deal with those sacrifices has a big impact on how we feel about our prospects for long-term success.

Catering

As an alternative to regularly scheduled part-time work, consider looking at a catering company. Many companies keep stables of staff available and schedule them when they need extra hands. They call you when they have an event scheduled and you see how it fits into your schedule. It's a great way to earn some extra money and try out the industry, without committing to regular hours. Many traditional temp agencies keep lists of experienced waitstaff on hand to call in a pinch. Once you've gained a little experience, contact a temporary employment agency to get your name added to the list.

If you live in a larger metro area, check Craig's List (www.craigslist.org) for part-time (and some full-time) job postings. All the listings are organized by city name, not by city and state. So, choose your city from the list on the right side of the screen, then all the listings on the left will correspond.

It's also handy if you're looking to relocate to another city; you can check out your job prospects in that locale ahead of time.

Seasonal Situations

Another great way to try out the restaurant business is by being a seasonal helper. Depending on where you live geographically (near a beach for example), one season (summer in this case) may be extremely busy due to an influx of tourists. Restaurateurs often bulk up their staffs for a set period of time just prior to those extremely busy periods, so that's a great time to have a short-term commitment to try out what might be your future career.

Summer Jobs

If you're a student, summer is your built in "try before you buy" season for any future career. It's a great fixed time that allows you to earn extra money and get a feel for the industry. Look for busy summer resort areas as prime summer job havens.

Remember, hiring for most summer jobs starts in April, so don't wait until the end of May to start looking and expect to land a great one. If you're looking at this job as a true test to see if you want to make a career out of this, take the time to find the right opportunity.

For help on getting a summer job at a resort, on a cruise ship, or other exotic food service locale, consider signing up with www.aplus-summerjobs.com. It's a nonprofit, subscription-based service (read as, it's not free), but it does boast excellent contacts in the resort world. And it doesn't accept money from the employers, so you are the client, not the corporation that has the most recruiting dollars to throw at it.

And remember, resort areas that are known for their winter activities have found ways to entice tourists in the summer, too. Ski resorts often cater to mountain bikers, hikers, and campers during the summer months. Don't miss out on those seasonal opportunities.

Holiday Help

Restaurants in busy shopping areas tend to need extra help around those all important holiday shopping hours. More people take days off to shop and have lunch, so days could be more busy than usual. With office parties, family get-togethers, and holiday engagements, more people celebrate those events in restaurants. Some restaurants expand their hours during the holidays, opening on Sundays in December, for example, to accommodate even more diners.

It may be a great time to think about a food service job that's not actually in a restaurant. Many bookstores have cafes and bakeries, and need extra help during the holidays. Or your local bakery may need kitchen help to complete its extra holiday orders. You can get some great experience "in the business" even if you're not in an official restaurant.

Try Out Different Service Styles

In order to make the transition from job to career, even if you have some restaurant experience, consider varying your experience to get a more well-rounded picture of what the industry is really like. Here's a list of ways to vary your experience:

- *Get a job in a casual or family restaurant.* Casual restaurants are, well, casual and can give you sort of a safety net when you're learning the basics of the business. If you don't serve from the left and pull plates from the right, very few people will notice. It's a great way to get started with just a smile and a positive attitude.

- *Get a job in a fast food restaurant.* You can learn a lot about cost controls, motivating employees, and being profitable in a fast food restaurant. In QSR, most managers make the workday into a game, racing against each other to see who can dress a burger the fastest. They watch the clock and do things like "stirring the restaurant" (stirring all the liquids such as sauces, dressings, and other toppings) on a specific schedule. It's a high-energy, controlled environment that can teach you more than you might initially imagine about the business.

- *Get a job in a bar.* Bars tend to have a different pace than restaurants. There's more variety in how involved you are with each party. Some are in the bar for 15 minutes, while others linger for hours. Some order food, some don't. So you'll start to hone your skills at reading guests and anticipating what they might need.

- *Get a job in a fine dining restaurant.* Fine dining is nonstop learning. The dining room atmosphere is typically very controlled, but a lot goes on behind the scenes that rarely is apparent to the guest. Working in fine dining is a great exercise in formality, preparation and planning, and reacting in a controlled way to inevitable stress. This step probably won't be first on your list, because without considerable experience, you probably won't get the job.

Experience Other Differences Before Buying Your Own Place

Before you plunk down your (or better yet someone else's) money to open your own restaurant, make sure you've rounded out your management experience by doing a few other things.

- *Switch sides.* If you have FOH experience, take a job in the BOH, or vice versa. Nothing is quite so eye opening as truly taking a walk in someone else's shoes. You can switch sides, so to speak, in your current restaurant or choose another. Either way, you'll be amazed at what you find. Hopefully, you'll see the challenges that the "other half" sees every day. You'll develop a more complete understanding of the whole of the restaurant.

You'll understand how vital communication is by making mistakes and seeing the consequences. See Chapter 9 for more information on using this experience to get ahead in the business.

- *Get a job in a busy restaurant.* Busy restaurants are typically run well, or they wouldn't be busy for long. Look at how they execute the volume they do. What systems work for them? How do they maintain their quality while they execute the quantity?

- *Get a job in a slow restaurant.* It may seem strange, but there's a lot to learn in a slow restaurant, too. In a slow operation, nothing gets covered up, and you have to be completely sound in your purchasing, in controlling your inventory, and iron fisted in your cost-control measures. In a nutshell, you learn how to wring every cent possible out of your budget in order to cover your expenses based on your volume.

- *Spend some time in a corporate-run restaurant.* A restaurant corporation can teach you a lot about the proper systems needed to run a profitable restaurant. They have systems for everything: training, handling personnel issues, maintaining proper sanitation, rolling out a new menu, controlling inventory. You name it; they have a system for it. And they make managers responsible for the individual store financials. You'll learn which numbers to watch for and what you can do to affect them. Even if you don't choose to implement the same systems in your own restaurant, you'll get thorough training in how they work, how to modify them to fit your needs, and why they are important.

- *Work in an independently-owned restaurant.* In a single-unit or independently run restaurant, you'll wear many more hats. If you are an assistant manager for example, you may be in charge of new employee orientation, contracting with the cleaning company, and hiring a company to repave the parking lot, in addition to your regularly scheduled duties as hall monitor and babysitter, I mean, floor manager and staff scheduler. You'll learn to think creatively as new situations arise. You'll become more flexible and quick on your feet. And you'll gain experience in just figuring stuff out as you go along. You'll likely be empowered to make more decisions than you would in a corporate environment, but you'll also face the consequences of those decisions.

SHADOWING/INTERNSHIP OPPORTUNITIES

Several useful web sites for finding a restaurant internship are:

http://internships.wetfeet.com/home.asp
Click on Search, then under Category Search, choose "Hotel & Restaurant." You can further customize your search by specifying the city and state where you'd like to find an opportunity.

www.jobshadow.org

Look for an office in your state to help you find job shadowing opportunities in your area. This organization offers more corporate participants and more hotels than freestanding restaurants.

www.restaurant.org/careers

The National Restaurant Association maintains a job database that can be checked out at their web site.

And remember, most degree and certificate programs include internship, externship, or apprenticeship opportunities.

Building a
Resume

He pursued an apprenticeship program and graduated with honors, then planned to move through the next five years of his career working in the best hotels available. This path was a common one, every new chef at the time knew that you must walk away from each experience with an honorable certificate to open the doors to the next level. Each time you do the best possible job you can, and then move up to a better hotel, and eventually, in 15 to 20 years, you might get to be an Executive Chef. In his particular case, Hans assessed his own strengths (making soups and sauces, for example) and weaknesses. He sought out opportunities to work intensely on his weaknesses, like cold kitchen skills and event planning. He took a job in Oslo, Norway, at the Hotel Bristol to do just that. He had an opportunity to cook for the Royal Family of Norway and gained experience planning parties many months out. During this time, he saw that there was much more to being a chef than cooking.

Several times in Chef Schadler's career, he was challenged to reach beyond his skill set and rise to the challenge of filling in for a superior for a temporary period of time. In one instance, it changed his life. He was cooking onboard a Norwegian American cruise line ship. His boss became sick and he became one of the youngest Executive Chefs in the company's history. At a very young age, he was in charge of 120 culinarians on the ship. This experience changed his outlook on life and his career. All at once, he had to shift from being "one of the guys" to being the boss, in charge of managing costs, food quality, and people he used to call friends. He spent five years in this position, but ultimately chose to leave the cruise ship lifestyle in favor of settling down and starting a family with his wife to-be, Liv.

When looking to add to his staff, Chef Schadler hires people with and without degrees. He says that, "Culinary schools today are remarkable, but also with remarkable price tags. So students feel the need to pay back [their loans] quickly. They want the money now," instead of building a resume and a career. Before going to school, he recommends that people seek out hands-on experience to get a feel for the hospitality industry. Also, he says people should consider pursuing "externships and intern programs in an intense professional operation. Use them as a stepping stone in your career." He suggests to look for an establishment that respects you, and does things right, one that's committed to an uncompromised team effort. This type of environment offers the best training for long-term success. Ultimately, he wants newcomers to, "Invest in your career, have a genuine desire and appreciation for what you are doing.

Chef Schadler also advises people new to the restaurant industry to, "Recognize that you don't have experience. Don't paint a different picture. Make a commitment to patiently and honestly build your career." Next, he recommends that new employees or apprentices should always ask questions. "You can't get answers if you are quiet." Finally, he says set realistic expectations, "Too many times, I feel like we're not spending enough time on painting the right picture [for students]. Schools do a great job, but expectations are a little too high when they step outside the classroom."

■　■　■

A resume is a great way to introduce yourself to a potential employer. It's a brief summary of your career life to date, placing an emphasis on your skills and experience related to the job you're trying to get. Many people skip this step when applying for a restaurant job, and in many ways, it's a mistake. If you are looking at this industry as a career, take the time to create a document that communicates that fact. Even if your resume is not extensive (yet!), it should be attention-getting and professional.

The exercise of writing a resume is a good one to do and do often, if just for yourself. Writing (and updating) a resume is a great way to

- focus your job search.
- figure out what you want to do now and in the future.
- sift through your experiences, and reflect on which ones might help you get your desired position.

- assess your skill set. (Note gaps that you can work to fill in.) It can help you get necessary experience to get your next job.

When applying to most restaurants, you'll need to fill out an application even if you have a resume. Make sure you bring the names, addresses, and phone numbers of previous employers or other references with you. Don't make them officially part of your resume, but have them handy. You'll need them.

Creating an Effective Resume

Writing a resume for this industry is similar to writing one for any industry. You list your quantifiable accomplishments clearly and succinctly. You note your specific expertise and quantify your accomplishments. If you're new to this industry, look at your skills and accomplishments and organize them in a way that will help a hiring manager know that you can succeed in this new-to-you venture. This section will show you how.

Resume Writing Basics

Always choose a standard, professional font between 9 and 12 point. You can go up to 14 or 16 for headings, if necessary. Resumes going to corporate restaurant companies are often scanned into databases, so using a simple font makes it easier for the scanner to turn your professional resume into searchable text.

Good font choices include:

- Times New Roman
- Book Antiqua
- Bookman Old Style
- Century
- Franklin Gothic Book
- Garamond
- Georgia
- Tahoma
- Verdana

Use **bold,** CAPITALIZATION, *italics*, and <u>underlining</u> to emphasize different points on your resume. But remember, the power of the emphasis lies in using these embellishments sparingly. You don't want to create the resume equivalent of a ransom note, by cutting **and** *pasting* *different* *fonts* together *word* **by** *word* *or* line-**by**-*line*.

At the top of your resume, list your name, address, contact number, and e-mail address. Even though the restaurant business has been notoriously slow in adopting technology, e-mail is highly useful during any job search. (You can get a free account at Yahoo!, Hotmail, or Google.) Because restaurant managers work some crazy hours, give them a way to contact you at their convenience, which could be 2 A.M., well beyond the reasonable telephoning-you-at-home time. And make sure you have a professional-looking e-mail address and appropriate outgoing voicemail message. No one wants to send mail to: Sam_and_Ella@badtummy.com.

In the restaurant business, you can skip the standard "Objective" section of the resume. (In fact, many recruiters advise everyone to leave this off resumes these days, but that's another book.) Instead, focus your time (and precious space) on highlighting a few achievements that you think will help potential employers see your value to them. If you're brand new to the industry, you want them to see that the skills you've developed in previous experiences can apply to your new chosen profession.

Here are a few examples:

- *Coordinated auditions for high school drama department, keeping track of 200 performers during two weeks of auditions for four productions per year.* This detail shows that you can function and stay organized in a highly dynamic environment like theater, or a restaurant.
- *Led sales team training at a retail clothing store, improving customer service by 28 percent.* This factoid shows a prospective manager that you place a priority on cus- tomer service, a must in the restaurant business, and can train for results.
- *Organized fundraisers for lacrosse club team, raising more than $5,000 over two seasons.* This entry shows that you have passion and dedication, and know how to work hard, like any successful restaurant professional.

Remember, don't worry about putting details, like dates, company names, and so on, in this section. You can do that below in the work history section. Instead, you're highlighting some of your qualities in hopes that the hiring manager will read on.

Specifics

Organize your work history in a logical way. If most of your experience has been with one company or in one position with several companies, choose how you want to highlight that. Group the information by the way you want employers to read it. Here are a few suggested organizational schemes.

Chronological. A chronological organization is pretty standard, especially if you're new to the job market. A hiring manager or HR representative can easily trace your career by looking at dates in one column and positions held in another. Descriptive text usually falls visually in between.

Summers 2003–present	**Indiana Oxygen Company**
	Administrative Assistant

- Maintained filing systems using Anacom barcode file management system.
- Shared responsibility for documentation of annual audit results with Controller.
- Provided efficient and courteous customer service to callers as documented by independent Mystery Shopper service.

1999–2003	**DePauw University**
	Computer Lab Technician

- Assisted students using Apple computers in new, state-of-the-art Macintosh computer lab.
- Responded to over 150 requests for assistance each week, with topics ranging from basic function overviews to macro creation, custom graphics applications, and the creation of advanced statistics and probability applets.
- Maintained firewalls and authentication protocols on university intranet.

Skill-Oriented. This format works well for people who have particular types of experiences they want to highlight for a potential employer, such as career changers or those new to an industry. In the case of the restaurant industry, I recommend highlighting customer service experience, sales experience, cooking experience (even if it's volunteer work at a soup kitchen, for example), performance experience, or management experience from another industry. It might look something like this.

Sales Experience
- Assisted customers with consultative sales support in the selection of makeup and other skin care items.
- Supervised the training of 12 new sales staff members from 1999–2001, using the proprietary *Haute Couture Guide to Cosmetic Sales*.

- Created bundled sales approach which increased sales of fall collection eye shadow duos by 15 percent over targeted projections during Q3 2001.

This type of experiential section is always followed somewhere on the resume by a brief employment section listing the companies you've worked for, positions held, and dates of employment.

Remember, in both organizational schemes, all the information is present; you just choose how you want to group it based on what you want the hiring manager to focus on.

Making the Most of Company Recognition

Including company recognition serves a very important purpose: it shows a hiring manager that your work was standout among a group of your peers. It says to a potential employer that you're the best of the best. You can work within and excel within the guidelines given to you by your managers and/or corporate offices. So in this industry, it says not only can you do the job but you also won't give your new managers a headache.

If you're fresh out of school, feel free to include prizes or awards won in your major. If you won your class' prize for best independent project, make sure you note it. If you were selected among the top in your graduating class, include that information. Any information that differentiates your resume from the others in the stack works to your advantage.

Quantifying Your Successes

Be specific when noting your achievements. Nobody cares if you "improved quality." But if you "increased customer satisfaction by 24 percent," people will notice. Paint a vivid picture for the hiring manager. Let them know that you were "responsible for grilling between 35 and 50 entrees per shift" rather than "ran the grill." Show them that you "improved add-on sales by 18 percent" instead of just "increased sales." Show them what you can really do; don't make them guess.

Your resume is your way to communicate that you are a solution to some problem a hiring manager has. Being specific in what results you can deliver is a sure way to make it to the interview and beyond.

Information about Professional Organizations

Membership in professional organizations shows that you are interested in learning as much as you can about your business. It reinforces the idea that you are independently responsible for your own destiny and career. It underscores for a potential employer that you are in the business as a career, not just a job. For more information on organizations in the industry that can help your career and your resume, check out the Appendix at the end of this book.

Positive References

Always offer references upon request. Do not list them on your resume, but be prepared to give names, titles, telephone numbers, and your relationship to each (neighbor, coach, former manager) when asked. (Note that family members are not good choices for references. Most hiring authorities assume that the information they get from family members is biased, so it's a waste to even include them as references.) You will be asked to write this information down on an application for an entry-level job. And you'll likely be asked to provide it for mid- to upper-level positions as well. For anything but entry level, the hiring manager may just call someone they know at your former company to see what they can find out about you.

Notice I said, "positive" references in the heading. Especially if you're new to a career, you want people who can attest to your general work abilities, like punctuality, attention to detail, work ethic, and so on. You may not have someone who can say, "He's the best cook I ever worked with," especially if you have no experience yet. But you want to include someone who can give positive, specific information about what a good addition you would make to the restaurant's team. Once you've been in the business for as little as six months or a year, you should have a few positive business references that can vouch for you. Personal references are only acceptable for a short time in the business world. Work on making a positive connection with people from the first day in your new position.

Remember, always get permission to use someone as a reference. Not only is it polite to ask their permission, but it also gives your contact an opportunity to mentally consider specific things he or she might say when asked about you.

Proofreading

Do not, I repeat, do not rely on spell check. It's a great tool that definitely has its place in the daily use category of technological innovations. BUT, it is no substitute for proofreading by a human being. Spell check will not pick up missing words, or misspellings that are actually words, but not the words you meant to type. (I'm notorious for misspelling homophones, like typing "their" for "there," and dropping letters, "you" instead of "your," for example.) Even a spell check program that includes a grammar check can miss this stuff.

A few resume proofreading steps can help you get the job done right:

- *Take at least a day between finalizing your resume and proofreading it.* Give yourself some distance from your work. Coming to your document fresh helps you spot errors.
- *Print out your resume, and review the hard copy.* I do most of my editing on the computer, but I always miss something. I consistently catch errors on the hard copy. It also gives you a chance to visually check the layout of the text. Make sure all your indents line up. Confirm your headings are formatted consistently. Verify that your document looks professional at first glance.

- *Read your resume backwards.* This step may sound strange, but it helps you focus on the mechanics instead of the meaning of the words. You can avoid assuming you know what the words say and actually see what they will say to someone else.
- *Read your resume aloud.* It slows you down. Often you can spot problems when you speak and hear them that your eyes might otherwise skip over.
- *Have someone else look over your resume.* This step gives you another perspective on your work and ensures that your thoughts are communicated clearly to someone else. Even professional writers (this one included) sometimes find that while they think they've written text that's crystal clear, they find out later, it's clear as mud to someone else.

Maintaining and Updating Your Resume

I can't stress enough how important this step is in building a resume over time. Take time to write down all the great stuff you do in your career. Note any training or certifications you've completed. Jot down any awards you receive (Employee of the Month, Manager of the Quarter, for example). Highlight any continuing education classes or seminars you've attended.

At least once a month, take the time to update your resume. At a minimum, jot down notes in your resume file, such as "received four outstanding comment cards this week."

Over time those notes will help you notice patterns in your work that can translate into powerful, specific bullets on your resume. It's absolutely critical that you do this at the time, rather than try to recall it all as you're putting together a resume a year later when you simply won't remember it all.

Sample Resumes for the Industry

To help you get started creating your own resume, I've included a few ideal resumes for different experience levels in both BOH and FOH positions.

ENTRY LEVEL RESUME—FOH

Greg Graduate
1122 Boogie Woogie Avenue
San Francisco, CA 94105
415.555.5555 m
415.555.6666 h
ggraduate@myschool.edu

Education

Berkley Institute of Art
    BFA—Drama, 3.89/4.0 GPA, Stage Production Minor, 3.54/4.0 GPA. Graduated with Honors 2004

Tom Collins' School of the Imbibery Arts
    Bartending Certificate, Spring 2005

Experience

- Lead roles in *Danny Boy, Othello, To Kill a Mockingbird, Cats,* and *Chicago.*
  - Played to over 2,000 patrons nightly from December 5 to December 15, 2003, during the BIA production of *Othello* at the Civic Center
  - "Greg Graduate's portrayal of Boo Radley was powerful beyond words." Sassy Liedigger, *San Andreas Faultfinder*
  - "Gus the Old Theater Cat was never so crotchety! Bravo, Mr. Graduate!" Milt Curmudgeon, the *Berkley Geriatric Theatregoers Review.*

- Stage Manager for adaptation of *Field of Dreams*, Spring 2002.
  - Coordinated a cast of 24 leads, 100 extras, and over 50 technical staff during a 12-show run
  - Managed staff of 10, including costume designers, make-up artists, and key grips

- President, Alpha Kappa Theta, Drama Society 2002–2004

- Internship, The Triton Hotel

- As part of Tom Collins curriculum, completed 6-month internship at the boutique Triton Hotel.

- Bartender, Barback
  - Created the Pomegranate-Passion Martini, winner, Best Martini—*CitySearch* 2004
  - Rotated through all bar positions, barback, service bar, bartender at trendy, 600 covers nightly Triton Club

ENTRY LEVEL RESUME—BOH

Candace Cook

592 Seminary Street
Greencastle, Indiana 46135
(765) 123-4567 home
(317) 765-4321 mobile

Highlights

- Educated in culinary arts and communications.
- Practical experience calculating food costs, event P&L, cash flow, and inventory valuation.
- Experience leading fellow culinarians in a task-oriented, brigade environment.

Relevant Skills and Experience

Culinary Arts

- Conceived and implemented Culinary Mentor Program for Culinary Institute of America (CIA), wherein students are paired with successful alumni via an e-mail "pen pal" support structure.
- Completed two school-sponsored culinary externships while at the CIA.
- Classically trained on all aspects of modern kitchen operation.

Organization and Leadership

- Assisted chef instructors with course presentations as a graduate teacher's assistant.
- Served as group leader and student council member at CIA.

Catering and Event Planning
- Helped prepare promotional materials for clients of public relations firm.
- Conceived and implemented promotional campaign for Culinary Institute of America (CIA) externship program with culinary magazines and journals.
- "Pitched" vacation packages for Country Inn and Resort in New York State.

Work History
- Test kitchen extern, *Good Taste* magazine, New York, NY, Spring 2000
- Cooking extern, Mama Rosa's Gourmet Market, Fishkill, NY, Fall 2000
- Caterer, self-employed, Albany, NY, and Poughkeepsie, NY 1995–1999
- Administrative assistant, Colby & Gruyere Public Relations, Albany, NY 1993–1995
- Promotions intern, Strawberry Fields Farms, New Paltz, NY Summer 1992
- Line cook, The Cider Press Tavern, Cortland, NY 1991–1992
- Server, Applejack's Cafe, Cortland, NY 1989–1991

Education
- Associate in Occupational Studies, Culinary Arts, The Culinary Institute of America, Hyde Park, Spring 2001
- B.A., English, State University of New York at Cortland, Cortland, NY Spring 1993

References available upon request.

MID-LEVEL RESUME—FOH

Marcy Manager
1234 Main Street
Wentzville, Missouri 65207
314.555.5555 m, 314.555.6666 h
marcy_manager@gmail.com

Summary of Qualifications

- Proven ability to manage diverse staff of 35 servers. Responsible for scheduling up to 10 stations, 2 shifts a day, 7 days a week.
- Maintained beverage program in a high-volume casual 250-seat restaurant. Responsible for purchasing, inventory, and promotions, for beer, wine and spirits programs. Increased alcohol sales 18 percent percent over 2 quarters.
- Developed and implemented training programs to improve guest service standards and increase add-on sales. Increased positive guest experience by 35 percent (as quantified by comment cards) and improved add-on sales by $2.80 per guest.

Professional Experience

The Italian Fisherman   **2000–present**

A high-end, independently owned 250-seat restaurant specializing in traditional Italian food and fresh seafood located in St. Louis, Missouri.

Dining Room Manager   2003–present
- Managed a staff of 35 wait staff, 8 greeters, 6 bartenders and other support staff.
- Revamped beverage program including purchasing process, inventory systems, and promotions for full service bar.

- Developed successful beverage promotions programs with coordinated staff training, resulting in increased alcohol sales of 18 percent percent over 2 quarters.
- Revised training programs using specific techniques to upsell food and beverages, increasing guest satisfaction (up 35 percent)and increasing add-on sales by $2.80 per guest over 6 months.

Server Captain   2001–2003
- Trained and evaluated approximately 15 new staff members each year on steps of service, menu knowledge, POS operations, and wine service.
- Led effort to revamp FOH cleaning schedules, including revised daily and weekly side work details.

Server   2000–2001
- Received "Outstanding" rating on 97 percent of customer comment cards.
- Won Highest Alcohol Sales monthly award 9 consecutive months.
- Received superior performance reviews in 2000 and 2001.

Juanita's Mexican Kitchen   **1997–2000**

Regional chain of 10 causal Mexican restaurants (each seating approximately 250 guests), operating in Columbia, St. Joseph, and St. Louis, Missouri, specializing in Tex-Mex cuisine, Mexican beers and tequila.

Corporate Trainer   1998–2000
- Interviewed and hired new staff members prior to opening 4 new stores in the Midwest.

- Developed training program for new employees in all front of the house operations, including the bar and the dining room.
- Trained more than 200 new staff members during 4 separate opening cycles.

Server/Bartender   1997–1998
- Efficiently served 10–45 guests per shift.
- Developed signature line of 8 margaritas, using high-end tequilas, fresh fruit juices, and other premium ingredients.
- Specialized in manning high-volume service bar, serving between 70–100 margaritas, 200–300 bottled and draft beers, and 50–100 cocktails per shift, 3 days a week.

Professional and Charitable Organizations

2003–present   Missouri Restaurant Association, member

2003   St. Louis Area Food Bank, volunteer

2000–present   National Restaurant Association, member

Education

University of Missouri-Columbia   1993–1997

Bachelor of Arts–English

References available upon request.

MID-LEVEL RESUME—BOH

Charlie Chef
1234 Main Street
Indianapolis, Indiana 46201
317.555.5555 m
317.555.6666 h
cchef@yahoo.com

SUMMARY OF QUALIFICATIONS
- Well-known chef in local and regional culinary communities with an extensive network of contacts.
- Proven ability to apply classic preparation methods in new, innovative ways with an eye toward quality and cost control.
- Proven ability to increase food quality and guest satisfaction while decreasing food and labor costs. Increased annualized gross revenue by 15 percent over forecast while lowering net food/labor costs.

PROFESSIONAL EXPERIENCE

2003–present   **Chef de Cuisine**
The Eagle's Nest, Hyatt Regency at State Capitol, Indianapolis Indiana
- Responsible for daily BOH operation and administration of a 150-seat, 4-star revolving rooftop restaurant averaging $1.4M+ annually in gross revenue.
- Led evolution of cuisine from traditional continental to innovative fusion cuisine with extreme success as quantified by guest response.
- Independently participated in active relations with purveyors, including research tours of specialty produce farms and seafood suppliers to maintain awareness of emerging trends.

- Won numerous awards for excellence and was featured in the May 2003 Restaurant Issue of *Indianapolis Monthly* as one of Indiana's most innovative young chefs.

2002–2003   **Sous Chef**
Herb 'n Things, Organic bakery and café, Indianapolis, Indiana
- Responsible for complete closing procedures nightly, including adherence to all sanitation process and security processes.
- Developed daily specials for 50-seat organic-only café.

2002–2003   **Chef/Owner**
La Petite Fete Catering, Indianapolis, Indiana
- Owned and operated independent catering company, geared toward events of 50 or fewer guests.
- Successfully completed 25 separate events, averaging 26 percent profit.

2000–2002   American Culinary Federation Apprentice
The Broker Restaurant, Denver, Colorado
- Trained by Chef Angelo Palmisano, C.E.C., on all facets of professional kitchen management and classical cuisine preparation techniques in a high-volume, 450-seat restaurant.

TEACHING EXPERIENCE

2002–present   **Chef Instructor**
                    The Corner Gourmet, Indianapolis, Indiana

2002–present   **Chef Instructor/Board Member**
                    Second Helpings Food Rescue and Job Training Program, Indianapolis, Indiana

2002	Advisor
	Ben Davis High School Area 31 Vocational Education Program, Indianapolis, Indiana

AWARDS AND RECOGNITION

2004	Manager of the Quarter, Hyatt Regency Indianapolis, 1st Quarter 2004
2003	Twice featured on The Television Food Network, *Cooking with the Corner Gourmet*
2003	Featured in *Indianapolis Monthly* magazine as one of Indianapolis' most innovative young chefs

MEMBERSHIPS AND CHARITABLE AFFILITATIONS

2000–present	Member, *International Association of Culinary Professionals*
2002	Member, *The National Ice Carving Association*
2000–present	Member, *The American Culinary Federation*

CULINARY EDUCATION

2000–2002	*The American Culinary Federation Educational Institute*
1999	*The School of Culinary Arts*, Denver, Colorado

OTHER EDUCATION

1994–1998	*DePauw University*, Greencastle, Indiana
	Bachelor of Arts—Emphasis in Political Science and Post-Secondary Education

REFERENCES AVAILABLE UPON REQUEST

Sample Cover Letter for a Job Ad

Read the job ad thoroughly. Reply to the ad specifically.

Job Ad

Job Description: McCoy's, America's finest steak-house, is conducting a nationwide search for a Chef!!! Chefs at McCoy's are responsible for executing consistent, high quality menu items by being hands on and working side by side with the kitchen staff, ensuring that each item is prepared to perfection. If you have a passion for service, commitment to uncompromising quality, strong attention to detail, appreciate the importance of following recipe specifications, and a belief that the best Chefs work on the line, not in the office—we want to talk to you!

This position offers full management benefits, including healthcare insurance, 401K retirement savings, paid vacation, and more!

Job Requirements: Two years of current hands-on kitchen management/supervisory experience required. Candidates for this position should have a strong sense of hospitality, be detail-oriented, and have the ability to work independently. Experience in a steakhouse setting preferred. Interested candidates please submit your resume to Herbert Humanresources, McCoy's Steakhouse, 5454 Elm Ave., Gaithersburg, MD, 20878, hhr@mccoys.com, fax 240-555-1212, phone 240-555-1414.

COVER LETTER RESPONDING TO THE AD

Charlie Chef

1234 Main Street
Indianapolis, Indiana 46201
317.555.5555 m, 317.555.6666 h
cchef@yahoo.com

Herbert Humanresources
McCoy's Steakhouse
5454 Elm Ave.
Gaithersburg, Maryland 20878

Dear Mr. Humanresources,

I was pleased to see your job posting at hcareers.com, soliciting candidates for a chef position with McCoy Steakhouse. I have a keen interest in continuing my career with a corporate steakhouse and believe I would be an excellent addition to your team.

I am an extremely hands-on chef, currently managing a team of 8 culinarians in my position as Chef de Cuisine. I work every shift on the line, in the trenches, making sure that our specs are followed, the quality of our food is excellent, and guest satisfaction is at an all time high.

Being part of a large corporation like the Hyatt has given me an excellent grounding in following corporate policies and recipe specifications and an opportunity to execute quality within those parameters.

I am open to relocating as necessary to pursue a position with McCoy's and am truly excited about McCoy Steakhouse's future plans. I have enclosed my resume for your review. Please contact me at your convenience to discuss my candidacy.

Sincerely,

Charlie Chef
enclosure

Unsolicited Cover Letter

Do your research. If they're not running an ad, they're probably not looking to hire anybody. You need to make them want to hire you anyway. Find out everything you can about the company, competitors, goals, expansion plans, and market segment so that you can tailor your letter to hit their hot button issues. Offer yourself as a solution to a problem that they might not even know they have. Use the internet, trade magazines, your network of industry professionals, and other resources to further your research. Note that research includes finding out to whom you send your resume. If it's an independent restaurant, you can usually find out by calling the restaurant and asking for the name of the person who does the hiring in the area you want to work in. The sample letter on page 138 is an example of how to phrase an unsolicited cover letter.

UNSOLICITED COVER LETTER

Marcy Manager

1234 Main Street
Wentzville, Missouri 65207
314.555.5555 m, 314.555.6666 h
marcy_manager@gmail.com

Ms. Angela Johnson
The Real Chili Factory
9876 West Bypass
Kansas City, Missouri

Dear Ms. Johnson,

I read about the upcoming opening of your second store in the Kansas City area in the May issue of *Missouri Restaurants on the Move* and must say, I am intrigued. I'm a member of the Missouri Restaurant Association and met your associate, Brad Beverage, at the annual trade show this spring. He was overflowing with enthusiasm for your restaurant concept, and it was contagious!

I'm currently looking to join the management team of a dynamic, up-and-coming restaurant company and believe The Real Chili Factory is just that company. I have enclosed my resume for your review. I have a proven track record for opening successful new stores, hiring and training large numbers of staff members in all areas of FOH operations, and for developing award-winning beverage programs.

I would love to discuss my qualifications with you and show you how I could be an immediately productive addition to your team. Please call me at your convenience to discuss.

Sincerely,

Marcy Manager
enclosure

Getting
Hired

When asked how she would describe her perfect candidate, Fox responds, "Passionate, energetic, well-groomed, articulate, and focused on what they want to do as well as eager and anxious to learn." She adds, "Lettuce [Entertain You] has a 49/51 hiring formula for new employees. The hiring decision bases 49 percent on the aptitude, experience, and ability of the candidate. Attitude counts for 51 percent. You can teach someone the nuts and bolts, but you can't teach them to be a people person."

Fox has been part of this industry for more than 20 years. During that time she's seen a shift in favor of pursuing industry-related degrees. She notes that restaurants, "no longer just put a sign in the window when they're looking for employees. Many people used to fall into the industry, working to pick up some money. These days, restaurants are using the same systems that other industries use, like recruiters and the internet." She also says that for the most part, "if someone is looking to make this business a career, they're getting a restaurant degree. More people are looking at this indus-try as if it's forever, instead of temporary."

Fox also offers a few tips on interviewing. "Don't interview right after you've lost a job or had a bad experience. Give yourself a week or so to get it out of your system." She also recommends that a candidate, "be energetic, even in your body language." She adds, "A sense of humor is a must."

■ ■ ■

G etting a job in the restaurant business is not terribly difficult. If you have a positive attitude, have good hygiene, are punctual, and are physically ambulatory, you'll likely be able to get an entry-level job. But if you want to find a job that's a bit more satisfying with advancement opportunities, job security, and extensive training programs, this chapter is for you.

Company Recruiting

Restaurants aren't so different from other businesses. They need people to fill all kinds of positions at all different levels. They use recruiters, the internet, and even newspapers to get potential employees in the doors. Here are a few of the best places to get the attention of the companies you want to work for.

Local Newspaper

Sometimes old school is the best way. If you need a job today, check out your local papers. Often they advertise current openings they need to fill immediately. It's not terribly high tech, but it works, especially for entry-level positions. Take a look at Chapter 4 for details on jobs at all levels in the industry.

Internet

Despite the fact that the restaurant business as a whole has been slow to embrace technology, the internet is a great place for soon-to-be restaurant employees to start looking for jobs. Several web sites cater to job seekers in the restaurant business, but as the hospitality industry continues to grow, more mainstream career sites are also getting in on the action. Most web sites are free to job seekers, at least at a basic service level. You can usually post your resume and search through opportunities by registering with the site for free.

www.hcareers.com. The "H" stands for hospitality. This web site is probably used by more restaurant job seekers than any other. In fact, all jobs posted through foodservice.com (a respected industry web site geared toward nonrestaurant foodservice, such as colleges, hospitals, and other commercial venues) and restaurant.org (web site for the National Restaurant Association), are available at hcareers.com (and vice versa). At the site's home page, you can choose from three focuses, hospitality jobs (which include FOH and BOH jobs in foodservice, in hotels, at resorts, on cruise ships, in the travel industry), restaurant jobs (which just focuses on restaurant and food-service jobs), and retail jobs. Once you choose your focus, you can then search for management or nonmanagement jobs, depending on your preference and experience level.

If you register with the site, you can post your resume (actually up to six different versions of your resume) immediately. Registration is free but requires that you have an e-mail address. Basically, you fill out a form that asks you questions about

- your contact information.

- your experience (including the number of years you've worked in the categories you've selected).
- work status in the country.
- any special skills (like large-volume cooking or opening experience).
- which languages you speak.
- what salary range you're looking for.
- when you're looking to start your new job.
- whether or not you're open to relocation (and how far away you're willing to go).
- your resume (you can actually cut and paste your resume into their form).

Employers search for candidates based on these criteria. If they choose you, then they can choose to look at your resume and contact you about positions they have available. Once you've registered, you can apply for any job you see on the site very quickly, with just a few clicks in most cascs, so you can be considered for the position immediately.

Another offering on www.hcareers.com is a "Job Detective" service. You fill out a form that describes the types of jobs you're interested in. The Job Detective e-mails you as new jobs matching your criteria are posted, enabling you to apply for them ASAP.

www.hospitalitycareernet.com. This site is much smaller than Hcareers.com (with career postings in the hundreds rather than the tens of thousands). But registration is free, so you might as well look here, too. It has a different set of resources, including an online skills assessment to help you find the right restaurant job. Its career advice is geared specifically toward the hospitality industry, not exclusively to the restaurant business.

www.careerbuilder.com. Careerbuilder.com is a huge job-search web site that has hooked up with other media (like newspapers) to provide a more all-encompassing employment search opportunity. It provides a resource center with all kinds of general job-hunting advice, like improving your resume, and articles on general career advice. It offers fee-based services that help you get your resume into the hands of recruiters in your industry.

While this site may have many job listings, it also has lots of advertising. "Business opportunities" abound, which isn't necessarily a bad thing, but just keep that in mind. You're not just looking at objective information on helping you get ahead in the business world here. Most of the information in its "Advice/Resources" section centers on recommending products to solve your job-hunting woes. Also, it's interesting to note that under its classification system, Hospitality-Hotel is a separate category from Restaurant-Food Service. Consider looking under both for restaurant jobs, because not all employers make this distinction.

Monster.com. Monster is one of the most well-known job web sites around. In fact over the last five or so years, it has swallowed up many smaller sites. Monster offers you a few options beyond the standard "post your resume/set up a job search service." It also offers networking services. You can search for people in your area (or an area you want to be in) with the same professional interests. And don't miss its blog http://monster.typepad.com/monsterblog for entertaining and applicable advice and general career talk.

While you're hunting for jobs online, don't forget the consumer restaurant sites. Most large cities (and many smaller ones too) have at least one web site that highlights the hot spots in your area. It may also highlight cultural events, happenings, and other tourist information. If your city has a consolidated restaurant web site to find restaurant reviews, menu prices, and make reservations, it may have a job board as part of the web site. Choose your favorite search engine and conduct a search for "[insert your town, state] restaurants."

Recruiters

When a company has a specialized position to fill, it hires recruiters (sometimes called head hunters) to bring it qualified candidates. Recruiters screen candidates based on the criteria the company has established for the job. Many recruiters keep in contact with candidates over a period of years, sometimes placing them with different companies several times.

For the most part, recruiters work with experienced hospitality professionals. If you're just starting out in the industry, you probably won't have the specialized skill set that companies pay to find. Once you've been around for a few years, consider contacting a recruiter to pair you with the right position.

Here are a few well-known hospitality recruiters:

The Hunter Group
480 Central Avenue
Northfield, IL 60093
Phone: (847) 441-6500
Fax: (847) 441-1111
www.hunt4job.com

Gecko Hospitality
119 East Ogden Avenue
Hinsdale, IL 60521
Phone: (630) 390-1000
Fax: (630) 390-0232
www.geckohospitality.com

T-A-Davis
604 Green Bay Road
Kenilworth, IL 60043
Phone: (847) 256-8900
Fax: (847) 256-8955
www.tadavis.com/

The Lucas Group
3384 Peachtree Road, Suite 700

Atlanta, GA 30326

www.lucasgroup.com/

Hospitality Recruiters

125 Habersham Drive, Suite C

Fayetteville, GA 30214

Phone: (678) 817-7220

Fax: (678) 817-7239

www.hospitalityrecruiters.com

Acing the Interview

Once you've made it to the interviewing stage, you want to get the offer. Much of the decision to hire you comes from the first few minutes (or seconds) of your interview. In fact, if a hiring manager decides *not* to hire you, that decision could well be made in the initial introductions. Once that decision is made, it's tough to turn the interview back around to your favor.

Passing the Screening Interview

Before you come into the restaurant (or corporate office) for an interview, you may be contacted by phone by someone who's screening applicants. This person is probably not making the hiring decision but facilitating the administration behind the decision. Ultimately, someone else will probably do the evaluative interview. In these mini-interviews, you may be asked to encapsulate your background, credentials, or your desire for the position. Or the screener may just be checking out how you communicate off the cuff. If you're caught off guard by the call, adjust your language and tone quickly to adopt an enthusiastic but professional demeanor.

Making a Great First Impression in Person

The first impression is a lasting one. In fact, if you don't make a good one, you won't get a chance to make a second. Here are a few tips on making the best first impression possible.

- *Be on time.* Late is not good. If you're late to an interview that should matter to you, how are you going to be on time to work?
- *Smile.* In this business, smiling is a must, even if you work in the BOH.
- *Be prepared to fill out an application even if you have a resume.* Many restaurants conduct background checks and require specific forms to complete them.
- *Dress for success.* No matter what the style of service, be well groomed and professionally dressed. Like it or not, you're in a business. Check out Chapter 2 if you need help.

Preparing for Questions

Take the time to plan answers to a few common questions. Practice your answers in the mirror. Don't make the answers sound memorized, but be prepared so that you underscore your professionalism, reinforce your goal orientation, and emphasize that you're self-motivated. Some sample questions are:

- Tell me about yourself.
- Where do you see yourself in 5 (10, 15) years?
- What's your passion?
- What do you want to get out of a job?
- What interests you about this company?
- When was the last time you were in here for dinner? What did you have? (And other follow-ups.)

Asking Good Questions

An interview is a two-way conversation. Both parties are looking for answers to questions and ultimately trying to make a good long-term match. Each party asks the other questions to determine whether or not they're a good fit. Asking questions in your interview provides you an opportunity to get answers to your questions *and* provides your potential employer with information about you. The questions you do (and don't) ask say a lot about how you might fit into an organization.

Here are some questions you should consider asking at your interview.

- *What are the long-term opportunities with your company? What's the anticipated career path?* Karen Fox says that these kinds of questions show that you're looking at this job as a career, with long-term potential. Because hiring a new employee is extremely expensive for a

company, it wants people who are serious about staying with it. Plus, you get the added bonus of knowing the answer to your question. Ultimately, future opportunity is a key factor in determining how happy (and for how long) you'll be in your position.

- *Is there an opportunity (or an expectation) for relocation?* Many corporate restaurant companies require eventual relocation in order for people to move up within the organization. If you're open to pursuing regional and multi-unit opportunities, you have a good chance of staying with the same company and continuing to grow.

- *What's a typical workweek like in your organization?* Ask this toward the end of the interview. "If you ask it early on," Fox adds, "You'll look like a clock watcher."

Following Up

It may sound quaint, but always follow up your interview with a short, personal thank-you note to your interviewer. Use it as another opportunity to place yourself as an ideal candidate for the job.

Follow these easy steps to create a memorable thank-you note.

1. *Thank her for her time.* Good manners go a long way in this business.

2. *Add a specific detail about the interview.* It personalizes the experience, showing that you have good attention to

detail and are invested in building a career with the company.

3. *Underscore your abilities and offer yourself as a solution to a problem it has, or remind her that you're a perfect fit for her team.*

4. *Provide a polite signoff as in the one below.*

Dear Ms. Palmer,

Thank you so much for the opportunity to discuss the bar manager position with you yesterday afternoon. I really enjoyed our discussion of your marketing plans for the upcoming holiday season. The ideas are innovative and energizing, and I know they'll lead to increased spirits sales.

With my extensive knowledge of single malt scotches, high-end brandies, and fine ports, I think I would make an excellent addition to your management team. I look forward to speaking with you again soon.

Sincerely,

Joey Jobhunter

TEN SURE-FIRE TIPS TO FIND THAT FIRST JOB

1. *Apply for a position during nonpeak hours.* Safe hours are 9:30 to 11:00 A.M., and 2:30 to 4:00 P.M. You may be offered an interview on the spot, so be ready.

2. *When you get an interview, be on time.* In fact, I recommend you arrive early.

3. *Smile!* It's an absolute must for this business. You'll be expected to smile from the minute you start your shift until the minute you clock out.

4. *Show you're full of energy.* The restaurant business requires long hours, often on your feet. Show the interviewer that you have the ability and willingness to get the job done well.

5. *Be yourself.* Let the interviewer see your personality. Don't feel you need to perform. Let her see what your skillset and unique view of the world could bring to the organization

6. *Eat in the restaurant before you apply.* Make sure you like it before free meals become part of your compensation package. Also, it saves you the embarrassment of not knowing how to answer when the interviewing manager asks you about your experiences in the restaurant.

7. *Show that you've done your homework.* Do your research ahead of time and look for opportunities to share the information you've gleaned. You should know general things about the restaurant (like what kind of things are on the menu, the style of service, and how many units they operate) and specific things (like the general manager's name).

8. *Don't put yourself above any job.* Many chefs started out as dishwashers. Lots of GMs worked their way through the ranks. No start is insignificant. A restaurant truly functions as a team. Everyone plays a vital role. Any experience is a learning one, so take advantage of everything you can in each position you hold.

9. *Make a friend at the restaurant who can give you the inside scoop and introduce you to a manager.* You'll have a leg up on the competition.

10. *Send a thank-you note.* Always. Some people won't consider hiring anyone that doesn't send a note. Others will remember you because you may be one of the few who sends one. Either way, you're ahead.

CHAPTER 9

Getting
Ahead

PROFILE

Chef Andrew Dismore

Corporate Executive Chef for
New Product Development and
Innovation, Noble and Associates
Food Marketing Company

A funny thing happened on the way to law school . . . Chef Dismore
discovered the restaurant business. After graduating from DePauw
University in Greencastle, Indiana, with a B.A. in political science,
Andrew made his way out to Colorado. As many people do, he got
a job in a restaurant because he thought it would be fun and pay

well. Little did he know he would find his passion. He worked as an apprentice rather than going through a certificate or a degree program in the culinary arts. Throughout his career he's gone back to school to concentrate on specific skills and interests, including taking courses at Le Cordon Bleu in Paris and at the CIA, both in New York and at Greystone.

Although he has no regrets about his own path and education, he recommends newcomers to the industry consider getting industry-specific degrees, saying, "It opens so many doors for you. Some companies and hiring personnel put a great deal of importance on the degree. Even though you can look at all the great self-taught chefs in the world, it's their passion, innate desire that brings them to greatness."

In his current job as corporate executive chef for new product development and innovation for Noble and Associates Food Marketing Company, Dismore hires both degree-holders and self-taught professionals. He believes in "kicking the tires." As he points out, "You can come from the best schools and graduate with honors, and I'm still going to want to see what you can do in the kitchen in a brigade environment. All the credentials in the world don't mean you can practically translate that to the requirements of the job and that you're able to co-exist in a stressful, dynamic, pressurized environment, like the kitchen." He adds, "I would rather hire someone with a willingness to learn the profession, who has a passion for the profession, than someone with a degree and an overinflated sense of self-worth and a sense of entitlement."

One of Chef Dismore's biggest surprises about the restaurant business is, "How much of the iceberg lies under the water, or how much of the industry the public isn't familiar with. It's easy to see the restaurants and hotels. Those usually come to top of mind when someone is considering [entering] this field, but after you're in [the business] for awhile, truly immersed in it, you begin to see the other opportunities and career paths others have taken. This business is continuing to evolve. New career paths are being created. Catering and the world of contract food service are massive. Whether it's a stadium or an arena, a college or a corporate campus, each has its own unique opportunities within the food service industry, in both the front and back of the house."

"I'm also surprised by how far you can go and how fast you can succeed if you're able to blend the tradecraft (ability to cook or serve) with basic business acumen, communication skills, a sense for marketing, and an understanding of basic economics and accountancy. Those attributes can really propel your career. I think I'm fortunate in my circuitous career path; coming from a highly recognized liberal arts school, like DePauw, really gave me a solid foundation upon which to build a career. I blended those skills with a true passion for this business."

For people considering entering the restaurant business, he recommends, "Put a toe in the water before you jump in with both feet. I encourage those just coming in to get a job in a large hotel. By hotel, I'm talking about a four- or five-diamond property that offers many outlets of service, styles of cuisines and numerous FOH and BOH possibilities for experience and growth. On a single property, you're able to find out a lot about everything, QSR to catering, breakfast dining to the highest of fine dining, all while having the stability and benefit of a corporation that offers insurance, vacation, retirement, and other employee benefits you won't find in most stand-alone restaurants."

■ ■ ■

There's a big gap between doing something and doing something well. If you're reading this book, I'm guessing you want to do this well. And in business, success is often defined by moving up in an organization. Getting more information, continuing to learn your business, and actively participating in the day-to-day operations can help you succeed. In this chapter, I offer you lots of hands-on advice for moving along on your quest to further your restaurant career.

Ask Questions, Always

No matter where you work in this business, you are constantly learning. Things are constantly changing. In fact, the dynamic environment is what draws many people to the business and keeps them here. Questions are a great way to get answers. Stop your trainer, your manager, the chef, or whoever you've working with, and ask questions on a regular basis. If you're in the middle of a hectic situation, hold your question until the rush is over, but don't forget it. If it's feasible, carry a notepad with you to jot down questions as you have them. Then, set aside regular time with a supervisor or mentor to discuss them. Don't feel like a dork. Many successful people use this technique.

You can't get a full picture of something until you've looked at it yourself, analyzed it based on your experience, and then filled in the gaps by getting answers to your questions. You can't learn anything from what you don't know. Most people in training positions agree that there's not a bad question, except the one that goes unasked. If someone objects to answering questions, you probably don't want to work for him.

Make sure you temper your natural curiosity with a sense of timing. If you're in the midst of a busy moment, measure the urgency of your question against the urgency of the moment. If you're pretty sure that the woman at Table 5 said she was allergic to shellfish and you're about to take her a plate of steamed mussels, you probably want to confer with someone ASAP. If you're curious about whether or not the new sage curtains were purposefully designed to accent the fresh colors of the chef's cuisine, you might want to wait to discuss that after the rush.

Stay Informed

When it comes to staying on top of industry news and food trends, you can't get too much information. And lucky for you, there's no shortage of ways to collect it.

Magazines and Newspapers

Periodicals are by definition updated often, usually weekly or monthly in the restaurant business. The trade magazines are great for staying abreast of current trends, but don't overlook what your customers are reading, too. Here's a list of my best picks to get you started. Look at both consumer and trade publications.

- *Nation's Restaurant News* (www.nrn.com). NRN is a weekly newspaper. It offers content at its web site as well, but you must be a subscriber to the hard copy newspaper to read some of the web articles. Check out its free targeted e-mail newsletters to help stay abreast of developments, like innovations in marketing for restaurants and beverage trends. I know some managers who make it required reading for their staff members. It's chock full of industry information, with articles on who's who, innovations in the industry, and other insider news.

- *Food Arts.* It bills itself as *the* magazine for food professionals. It offers lots of information, including profiles of chefs, recipes, and food trends. It also covers some restaurant-specific interior design topics. Definitely try this one out, especially if you think you want to focus on the BOH.

- *Restaurants & Institutions.* This magazine supports restaurants (from coffee shops to the fine dining restaurants on the lake) and institutional foodservice venues (like university cafeterias or hospitals). It provides case studies, profiles of business success stories, and trend information. Check it out online at www.foodservice411 .com/rimag.

- *Consumer publications.* Read consumer-focused publications, like *Bon Appetit, Wine Spectator,* and *Gourmet* to have more insight into what customers are expecting from you and your restaurant.

Go to www.tradepub.com and look at its Food and Beverage section to find several helpful magazines (including *Food Arts* and *Restaurants & Institutions*). Apply to see if you qualify for some of these resources for free. You'll go through a lengthy registration process, but it's worth it. And just a note, you're more likely to qualify for the free subscription if you're involved in purchasing decisions at your restaurant.

Books

Although they are not so regularly updated but still great resources to keep on hand for a budding restaurateur, here are my top picks for books that you should keep in your library:

- *The New Food Lover's Companion* by Sharon Tyler Herbst (Barron's Education Series). I refer to this book constantly whether I'm writing or reading about food. It's packed full of 6,000 culinary and dining terms to help you in your day-to-day work with food. It's a must-have for anyone who's serious about a restaurant career.

- *Service That Sells! The Art of Profitable Hospitality* by Phil Roberts (Pencom). This book is a FOH must-read. It gives excellent advice on selling food, not taking orders. Using the information in this book, you can make more money immediately in tips and more money in the not-so-long run for your restaurant.

- *Running a Restaurant For Dummies* by Michael Garvey, Heather Dismore, and Andrew Dismore (John Wiley & Sons). This entry is not *just* a shameless plug for a book I co-authored. It's also a great introduction to the restaurant business from inside the restaurant. It's different from this book in that it's about the restaurant itself, how it works, how you can make it work better, and how you can make money doing it. It provides great hands-on, make-a-difference-in-your-current-restaurant-today information, but it does assume that you're in a decision-making place in the restaurant. Even for total newbies, I think it's a good read because it gives you basic information on things to watch for in the restaurant (like sanitation or menu writing and design) that you might otherwise miss.

Web Sites and Web Logs

Ah, the internet . . . and to think we're just a few short years into its history in the mainstream. It's truly among the most helpful tools for anyone doing research on just about anything. Of course, the challenge isn't finding information, it's finding *reliable* information. I've done part of that work for you. Here are a few of the sites I use regularly to keep up on what's going on in the world of food.

- *Foodservice 411* (www.foodservice411.com). Requires a lengthy registration, but you get immediate access to lots of interesting stuff, including rankings (like the Top 100 independent restaurants) or tips for driving traffic to your restaurant. It's a consolidated site featuring content from the teams that bring us *Restaurants & Institutions*, *ChainLeader*, and *Foodservice Equipment & Supplies*.

- *RecipeSource* (www.recipesource.com). For the sheer volume of stuff there. It has a recipe for everything. No seriously, I mean everything. If you find the site useful, it has a "click-to-pay" button that you can use to toss them a dollar.

- *The Restaurant Report* (www.restaurantreport.com/ index.html). Offers good basics of the industry. It might not have the latest trend info, but I like its fundamentals.
- *Luxist.com*. A *blog* (short for web log or online journal). It focuses on high-end luxury items and info. Information about an over-the-top restaurant (like the new coffee house just opened by Gucci) or food trends (like the best and worst in airport cuisine) can be found here. And, to be honest, it's sort of a guilty pleasure to read about even the nonrestaurant luxury information. Read at your own risk of becoming disenchanted living down here with rest of us peasants.
- *Slashfood.com*. Full of fun, quirky bits of foodie heaven. It's also a blog, where you can respond to articles you read and connect with other users of the site. It even has a section of the site dedicated to restaurants. Log on and enjoy.

Get Involved

Get involved with your community and industry. Besides being a good thing to do, you can make great contacts that could be a key part of your future success.

Attend/Host Charity Events

Many communities have charity events focused on food. You've probably seen them. Local restaurants set up booths in a shopping mall, convention center, or hotel banquet facility. They hand out samples of a few of their signature dishes.

Attendees buy a ticket to attend and sample the wares. The price of the tickets is donated to the charity. The restaurants donate their time and product to the cause.

Being part of these events is great, whether you're an attendee or a participant. As a participant, you can mingle (a bit) with your fellow restaurant people, usually while you're setting up and tearing down. You can pick up on "buzz" in the crowd, getting the 411 on what's good, what's bad, and what's, well, weird. And it's all for a good cause.

Join Trade Associations

Trade associations are built-in networks of people with quite a bit in common—their livelihoods. Trade associations are typically made up of people with interests in a specific industry. In the restaurant business, it's restaurants (duh) and their employees, people who service restaurants (like equipment purveyors or chemical specialists), students learning the trade (special student rates often apply), faculty members, and nonprofit groups with an interest in the industry.

Look for national and state associations that fit you best. You can find a listing of recommended organizations (and their contact information) in Appendix C.

Expand Your Work Horizons

As I've mentioned several times in the book, self-motivation and hard work are two key traits of every successful restaurateur. No matter what your experience level in the business, you can almost always do more, learn more, and achieve more. Here are a few ideas for taking your training into your own hands and making the most of every work situation.

Volunteer for Extra Work

By volunteer, I don't mean to imply that a restaurant is a charity that deserves your services free of charge. I mean, set yourself up as the go-to person when it needs extra shifts picked up. Take on extra projects, like reorganizing dry storage on a Monday morning. Lead the effort to get people excited about new menu offerings. Whatever your circumstances, have your superiors look at you as a leader among the staff. Sooner or later, probably sooner, they'll need you to step up officially and lead.

Job Shadow Other Positions

It pays to know how to do other people's jobs. What happens when the oven guy doesn't show up for his Saturday lunch shift? If you know how to make the pizzas, you could save the day. Or maybe the pantry gets slammed with a busload of dinner salads. If you're able to slide over and help out during the rush, you win.

And the prize isn't just looking good to the managers. If you can perform multiple duties, they can send other people home during slow times, but you can stay and get extra experience, hours, and money.

Offer to Stay Late and Come in Early

Make your managers' lives easy whenever possible. Don't give up your personal life (there'll be plenty of time for that once you're actually *in* management), but don't try to jet out of the restaurant as soon as your shift's over. Likewise, don't glide into the restaurant just in time to clock in. Show your professionalism by arriving on time and staying until all the work is done. Your reliability and diligence will be rewarded.

Stay Close to Your Guests

This business is completely based on satisfying the guests. Talk to them often about their experiences, their meals, and their lives. And more importantly, *listen* to your guests. They have lots to say, maybe more than you'd like to hear some days. But over time, you'll develop a filter that separates small talk from true honest to goodness feedback that you can use to improve your service and the restaurant.

It goes without saying (I hope) that inside the restaurant, this little nugget of advice only applies to people who have typical contact with the guests. It would probably not appropriate for a prep cook to come out of the kitchen to check in with a diner to see that the romaine was chopped to her liking. On the street, feel free to talk to whomever you want about their experience in the restaurant, whether you're in the BOH or FOH.

Get a Second Job

Double your experience, double your fun. If you're in a management position, this one is probably not a viable option because you'll not have the extra time to get a second job. But if you're an hourly employee, you can increase your experience (and bank account) by getting a second job in the industry.

Work in a Hotel

A hotel is an excellent place for a would-be restaurateur to work. You get to experience all different kinds of dining, all under one roof, or at least just a few roofs really close to each other. The hotel may have several restaurants, banquet facilities, and room service. Each venue has its own set of menus, logistics, challenges, and systems. If you want to run your own show one day, you'll get a boatload of experience in a hotel.

Work for a Caterer

Caterers excel at serving lots of people in a short amount of time. Catering is truly an art. Not only do caterers have to know how to prepare great food, caterers also need to know

- how much food to actually prep so they have enough to serve, but not too much to waste.

- how to prepare a new menu for a new clientele every night.
- how to set up and tear down full dining rooms and (sometimes) mobile kitchens.
- how to serve buffets, receptions, and plated multi-course meals to parties of 10 to 10,000 guests at a time.
- a host of other logistical challenges.

The experience will be invaluable, and you may find out that you prefer the pace of this foodservice specialty. See Chapter 6 for other tips on jobs to try to move your career along at your own pace.

TEN TIPS TO SUCCESS IN THE INDUSTRY

1. *Take responsibility for your own career.* Don't expect that anything will be given to you. Seek out learning opportunities. Network with your peers. It's the right thing to do for *you.*

2. *Set goals and review them often.* Don't be intimidated about writing them down. Set timelines for achieving them. Look at them often, because as you learn more about your business, you're likely to have more realistic incremental minigoals that can help you achieve the big ones. Goals are not set in stone; they can be revised at any time. Remember, "goals are just dreams with a deadline."

3. *Go the extra mile.* "Good enough never is." If you're reading this book, then you know that to reach your full potential, you have to go beyond the basic requirements. You need to push yourself to exceed even your own expectations. Do it in this business, and people will notice.

4. *Don't be afraid to sell yourself.* Confidence is not a dirty word. You can be assertive without being pushy.

5. *Get involved in your community.* Doing something good for your neighbor is never a bad thing.

6. *Remember, it's a small world.* Never burn bridges. You never know when you might need help from someone you used to work with or worked for. Always leave a position on good terms.

7. *In the beginning, choose positions for the experience; the money will follow.* Don't be immediately concerned with the money. Get the fundamentals of the business down. Know your stuff, and within a matter of a few years, your paycheck will catch up to your aspirations.

8. *Continue to develop your skills.* You should be constantly looking for your weaknesses. Look for skills you're missing, training you need, or areas to work on.

9. *Seek out a mentor.* Look to someone in the business you respect and admire. Take her out to lunch, or buy her a cup of coffee. Pick

her brain about potential career moves. Talk to her about trends
he's seen come and go. Have her look at your goals and timelines
in order to help you set appropriate expectations.

10. *Build a network of peers.* A network can help you find the perfect
job, find good employees, seek out new vendors, and even lend
you products when you're in a bind and your vendor's warehouse
is closed.

Make It on
Your Own

PROFILE
Rick Enos
Compadres Bar and Grill

The Compadres is a general partnership of
Rick Enos and Richard Bradley. They operate
several dining venues in Hawaii and California, including
Compadres Bar and Grill (with locations in Honolulu, Maui, Palo
Alto, and Oakland). With a third partner, Joel Trammer, they own
another location in Yountville (Napa Valley), California. In addition to
their freestanding restaurants, they operate taqueria style and kiosk
operations at SBC Park (home of the San Francisco Giants), Monster

Park (home of the San Francisco 49ers), Aloha Stadium, and University of California–Berkeley Memorial Stadium.

With annual sales topping $10 million companywide and nearly half a million guests each year, there's a lot for these guys to celebrate. And they do. Serving up their "Western Cooking with a Mexican Accent," they pride themselves as the "wedding rehearsal dinner capital of the West" at their Yountville location. Their beverage program sports an award-winning wine list and margaritas, and that's saying something in Napa Valley wine country. The ambience is festive and fun; they describe it as "contemporary design accented by Mexican artifacts."

All locations serve the same menu for lunch and dinner daily. Maui and Yountville also serve breakfast. Compadres trains all its culinarians, rather than looking for culinary school grads. The owners are focused on consistency and excellence throughout their operation, so they teach people what they need to know to succeed in their restaurants.

Rick Enos oversees the operations from his office in San Rafael, California. He supports his managers in the office, so they can focus on the floor, both the FOH and BOH as necessary (FOH stands for front of the house, which is anywhere a guest can see; BOH means back of the house, which is anywhere a guest can't go, such as the kitchen). He also physically oversees most of the larger catering events. Rick loves the restaurant because, "It's the only business that I know of where every facet of business—ordering, inventorying, planning, production, sales, service, and consumption—takes place in one place in a short period of time." He also enjoys the unpredictability of the business. It really adds to the challenge. He loves "seeing and hearing from totally satisfied guests whose expectations we have exceeded."

He tells all his managers to "end the interview" if the prospective employee doesn't smile within five seconds. He thinks all employees of the restaurant should entertain the guest "as a true host." He advises newcomers to the industry, "Do not take yourself too seriously! Have fun!" He looks for employees that are "team players [who] like to have fun, [aren't] afraid of hard physical work, are slightly irreverent, and have charm and wit and [know] how to use each to their/our advantage. Hospitality should come easy to them." He also notes, " I hate to hear the sound of dragging feet in our restaurants. I want people who have a good sense of self-worth and who take pride of ownership in what it is that they are doing. I like decision makers, and people who take responsibility for their decisions."

■ ■ ■

The restaurant business is the ideal business for an entrepreneur. Each and every day you have to make adjustments to your plan, based on the guests coming in the door. Exceeding their expectation is the key to reaching your goal. You have to actively manage the business in order to succeed and ultimately profit.

This chapter discusses ways to approach the business as an entrepreneur. It requires previous experience (and lots of it) to be successful.

Check Out Entrepreneurial Opportunities

Webster's New World dictionary defines an *entrepreneur* as "a person who organizes and manages a business undertaking, assuming the risk for the sake of a profit." You may not be ready to assume all the risk for a new business, but this section discusses ways to make the restaurant business your own, identifying the pros and cons of each option.

Buying a Franchise

Many restaurant chains operate as *franchises*. That means someone (a *franchisee*) has bought a license from the restaurant company (or *franchisor*) to sell the restaurant's food and use its brand, logos, and name. Most restaurant companies have a mix of company-owned and franchised stores. Big names in the franchising world are McDonald's, Wendy's, and Applebee's.

Some benefits of having a franchise are:

- The franchisor does a lot of the legwork, (such as market research and analysis and menu development). It has marketing and a promotions team in place, often with national advertising plans. It also has many in-store marketing materials and displays for you to use.
- The franchisor should already have a solid clientele base, recognizable brand identity, and familiar menu items. The consumer already knows them and how to use the brand.
- The franchisor should have lots of systems and controls in place for you, such as purchasing, rotation, and sanitation systems.
- The franchisor should give you a full set of human resources and administrative policies and forms.

One important point is that the more expensive the franchise and the more well-known the franchisor is, the more systems and support you get. If you're thinking about signing up with a newer, less well-known (and less expensive) franchise, make sure you know exactly what you're getting and what it will cost you.

Some of the negatives are:

- If you're looking for creativity, you probably won't have it with a franchise. Because it's selling you a license to sell its products, it controls much of how you do that.
- You have to pay regular franchise fees (usually monthly) and often a percentage of sales as well, right off the top . . . and they get theirs, no matter what.

- Depending on the franchise you go with, the start-up fees can be high, and you may have to agree to open multiple stores in your area within a short time. Also, very often you must have *a lot* of liquid capital to qualify as a franchisee.

Buying an Existing Restaurant

Whether you are looking at buying a restaurant you're currently working in or one you're not affiliated with, find out why the owner is selling it. If, for example, the owner is retiring or relocating to another state, he probably has no ulterior motive. But if he's getting out of the business for any other reasons, warning lights should go off for you. Don't get stuck with a lemon.

Some reasons to buy an existing restaurant:

- You could have an instant client base to build on.
- You could have a successful infrastructure (like trained employees, all the right equipment, and established vendors) in place.

Some reasons not to buy an existing restaurant:

- The restaurant may not be profitable for a variety of reasons. Make sure you do a thorough examination of the books with an independent auditor or other financial analyst.
- The physical plant of the restaurant may have problems. Make sure you inspect the property thoroughly with a trusted contractor before finalizing the deal.

- You are buying the restaurant, but not the property. If you are agreeing to assume a lease agreement, have that contract analyzed by a qualified attorney. Often leases end and if you choose to exercise your option to renew, the lease may have doubled or tripled. *Always* have your contracts, leases, books, and any binding documents reviewed by a qualified professional.

This list is very basic. Definitely do lots of research on any business venture that you're considering being part of.

Starting a Restaurant

For many people, this is the ultimate goal. It can be a very alluring fantasy, but do not, I repeat, *do not* take this step until you are beyond ready. I know quite a few people who have lost everything, not because they weren't talented and smart, but because so many factors go into successfully starting a restaurant, not the least of which is money. No one person can expect to be the master of all the disciplines that go into owning and operating a successful restaurant venture. You need qualified, objective partners (your brother-in-law does not count) who can give you sound advice and help ensure your success.

Now that I've totally scared you off, let's look at the upside of starting your own restaurant:

- You can truly make it your own. Good, bad, or ugly, you're in charge, so run it your way.

- You can build the physical space to suit your menus, style, and taste.
- You have the satisfaction of creating your own success.
- You can take all the risk and reap all the reward.
- You are your own boss

The reasons not to start your own restaurant are:

- You have to build the business from scratch. You have to establish your brand identity, steal market share from the competition, and continue to retain and grow your following.
- You have to play many roles and have a plan to cover for your weaknesses. You are often pot-scrubber and CEO. You will work harder and longer than you initially imagine. Make sure your personal and family life can take the hit.
- You will have to develop your own human resource systems. Like any other business, a restaurant can be a target for lawsuits, usually sexual harassment or wrongful termination, so make sure you have systems in place to document everything.
- Restaurants are capital intensive. Know that you will have to put personal guarantees on just about all your financing. So if the business goes under, you personally will still be on the line for repaying much of the debt. Get a good accountant and attorney, and before all the paperwork is done, know what the worst-case scenario is going to be and make sure you can live with it. Most

restaurants fail due to undercapitalization. They are not able to withstand the business-building phase. The lack of cash flow is the killer.

Look at Freelancing

You can find quite a few freelance opportunities supporting the restaurant business. Many opportunities allow you to run your own show without the capital investment in a restaurant. This section gives you an introduction to a few of them.

Consulting

If you're leery to jump in with both feet and run your own place, consider helping other people run theirs. *Consultants* tell people in the industry how to do their jobs better, more efficiently, and more profitably. They charge a fee for their services, sometimes with a bonus based on achieving specific results. Consultants are typically not full-time employees but rather are contracted by a restaurant to look at a specific aspect of its operation and solve a specific problem or make a specific improvement.

Here are just a few kinds of consulting services currently available in the restaurant industry:

- *Menu development and analysis.* Two basic categories of menu developers exist, those with culinary backgrounds and those with graphic design backgrounds. They examine your menu and review it, looking at things like:

- *Menu synergy.* Do your menu items require the optimal number of inventory items? For example, does it require you to keep three different kinds of canned tomatoes (stewed, crushed, and diced) when just using one (say, crushed) might work more profitably. They can help tweak your menu by adding items, using ingredients that you already use regularly, in a new and interesting way.
- *Menu profitability.* They analyze your menu to see what's selling, how much you are making from each entrée, and look for ways to improve it.
- *Menu engineering.* Basically, they look at how the menu is laid out graphically. They help you place your most profitable items on the most-often viewed spots on the menu, increasing sales of those items and, ultimately, increasing your profits.
- *Food trends.* Some consultants watch food and dining trends. They advise clients who are looking to update their menus stay ahead of the trend curve and match their customers' expectations.

• *Efficiency review and improvement.* These consultants look at how orders and people flow through the restaurant. They often look at the physical setup of the restaurant and offer advice on improving it. Many of these consultants also provide overall operations assistance too.

• *Service refinement.* A service consultant works with the FOH staff on the finer points of serving guests. They may offer advice in clearing dishes, upselling items, greeting people at the door, and the like.

- *Operations assistance.* These consultants specialize in the day-to-day running of the operation. They look at your ordering procedures, vendor pricing, and inventory procedures. They may also look at the physical setup of your restaurant and look to improve efficiencies.

- *Start-up expertise.* Consultants are available to work through every phase of the planning of starting a new restaurant, including creating a business plan, negotiating a lease for the space, even developing the restaurant's concept, logo, and brand identity.

- *Alcoholic beverages (wine, beer, liquor).* If you need help in this area, alcohol vendors are the place to go. Usually they will offer free staff training (on their own products, of course) to educate staff about the finer points of their product lines and other beverage basics. Often they start with the basics (how beer is made, for example) and then progress to the nuances and subtleties of their products.

Work for a Staffing Service

Consider working for a hospitality staffing service. A caterer, for example, calls a service and "orders" help (like bartenders, servers, and cooks) for special events. The best thing about this system is that you get exposure to many different companies in the industry, so that you can see how they really work in the field and get a feel for how you might fit in to their organizations.

Industry-Related Support Jobs

Maybe you don't feel like the actual restaurant business is right for you. Maybe you want to be home more with your family, or you don't enjoy the hectic pace. Perhaps you just want to slow down a bit, for whatever reason. Many support positions can help you do just that.

- *Food sales.* Food vendors employ salespeople who go out to restaurants and introduce their products. These salespeople need to have a keen understanding of their own product lines and an understanding of the restaurant they're selling to. Their job is to show a restaurateur that their product line has value in the restaurant (maybe they can save money, improve quality, or offer a new product to their guests).

- *Alcohol sales.* Alcohol sales are very similar to food vendors, but they deal with beer, wine, and liquor. Their pitch usually focuses on pairing their beverages with the restaurant's menu, atmosphere, or clientele.

- *Marketing/public relations.* Many restaurants employ marketing or public relations people either as full-time or contract help. They may hire someone to create a mailing to get the word out about their new lunch specials or promote their happy-hour deals. Or maybe they need help reaching customers outside their immediate geographic area. Whatever the case, marketing restaurants is here to stay.

- *Special event planning.* These professionals are employed by restaurants to plan special events like grand openings. They may also work with restaurants on behalf of private clients to organize and plan events, such as wedding receptions, bridal showers, and holiday parties

- *Food styling.* Food stylists work with photographers to take beautiful pictures of food. These pictures are used in advertisements, on menus, in cookbooks, on web sites, and in just about any media format. The stylists arrange the food to get the most appetizing shots possible.

- *Food writing.* Food writers can write about food and restaurants in many different ways including:
  - Local restaurant reviews
  - Seasonal pieces on related foods
  - Interviews with food professionals
  - Transitional text (text between the recipes) for cookbooks
  - Copy for food advertisements
  - Blog entries for food web sites
  - Books, such as the one you're reading now

Schools for
Industry Degrees

Nationwide Schools

The Art Institutes
Campuses nationwide
Phone: (888) 624-0300
www.aii.edu/culinary

DeVry University
Nationwide campuses offering a Business Administration
degree with Hospitality Management concentration.
Phone: (866) 338-7934
www.devry.edu

Johnson & Wales University
(4 campuses nationwide)
8 Abbott Park Place

Providence, RI 02903
Phone: (401) 598-1130
http://culinary.jwu.edu

Le Cordon Bleu
Corporate Office
40 Enterprise Avenue
Secaucus, NJ 07094-2517
Phone: (800) 457-CHEF
Fax: (201) 617-1914
www.cordonbleu.edu
e-mail: info@cordonbleu.edu

Remington College
For Culinary Arts
1800 Eastgate Drive
Garland, TX 75041-5513
Phone: (972) 686-7878
Fax: (972) 613-3063

For Hospitality Management
1111 Bishop Street, Suite 400
Honolulu, HI 96813-2811
Phone: (808) 942-1000
Fax: (808) 533-3064
www.remingtoncollege.edu/index.html

Schools in the Northeast
Atlantic Culinary Institute at McIntosh College
181 Silver Street

Dover, NH 03820
Phone: (877) 628-1222
Fax: (603) 749-0837
www.atlanticculinary.com

Connecticut Culinary Institute
Main Campus
230 Farmington Avenue
Farmington, CT 06032
Phone: (800) 762-4337
www.ctculinary.com/index.htm
e-mail: admissions@ctculinary.com

Cornell University
School of Hotel Administration
Statler Hall
Ithaca, NY 14853
Phone: (607) 255-8702
Fax: (607) 255-9243
www.hotelschool.cornell.edu

Culinary Academy of Long Island
125 Michael Dr.
Syosset, NY 11791
Phone: (516) 364-4344
www.culinaryacademyli.com

Culinary Academy of New York
154 West 14th Street
New York, NY 10011

Phone: (212) 375-6655

www.culinaryacademy.edu

Culinary Institute of America (CIA)

Admissions Department

1946 Campus Drive

Hyde Park, NY 12538-1499

Phone: (800) CULINARY

www.culinary.edu

e-mail: admissions@culinary.edu

The French Culinary Institute

462 Broadway

New York, NY 10013-2618

Phone: (888) FCI-CHEF

www.frenchculinary.com

New England Culinary Institute

Green Mountain Building

Admissions Office

250 Main Street

Montpelier, VT 05602-4201

Phone: (877) 223-6324

www.neci.edu

e-mail: info@neci.edu

New England Technical Institute

106 Sebethe Drive

Cromwell, CT 06416

Phone: (860) 613-3350

or

8 Progress Drive
Shelton, CT 06484
Phone: (203) 929-0592
www.newenglandtechnicalinstitute.com

Pennsylvania Culinary Institute
717 Liberty Avenue
Pittsburgh, PA 15222
Phone: (412) 566-2433
www.pci.edu

Schools in the Southwest
Arizona Culinary Institute
10585 North 114th Street, Suite 401
Scottsdale, AZ 85259
Phone: (866) 294-CHEF
www.azculinary.com

New Mexico State University
Gerald Thomas Hall
Room 119, College Street
Box 30003, MSC 3HRTM
Las Cruces, NM 88003
Phone: (505) 646-5995
Fax: (505) 646-8100
http://hrtm.nmsu.edu
e-mail: hrtm@nmsu.edu

Scottsdale Culinary Institute
8100 East Camelback Road, Suite 1001
Scottsdale, AZ 85251
Phone: (888) 356-6666
www.chefs.edu

University of Nevada–Las Vegas (UNLV)
4505 Maryland Parkway
Box 456013
Las Vegas, NV 89154-6013
Phone: (702) 895-3161
Fax: (702) 895-4109
http://hotel.unlv.edu

Schools in the West
California Culinary Academy
625 Polk Street
San Francisco, CA 94102
Phone: (800) 739-9700
www.baychef.com

California School of Culinary Arts
521 E Green Street
Pasadena, CA 91101
Phone: (626) 403-8490
www.csca.edu

California State Polytechnic University–Pomona
The Collins School of Hospitality Management

3801 West Temple Ave. #79b
Pomona, CA 91710
Phone: (909) 869-2275
www.csupomona.edu/~cshm/collins_school/index.htm
e-mail: Cshm@Csupomona.edu

College of Southern Idaho
Evergreen Building
315 Falls Avenue, P.O. Box 1238
Twin Falls, ID 83303-1238
Phone: (800) 680-0274, ext. 6407
Fax: (208) 736-2136
www.csi.edu/l4.asp?hospitality

Culinary Institute of America at Greystone
2555 Main Street
St. Helena, CA 94574
Phone: (707) 967-1010
www.ciachef.edu/california
e-mail: wsgr@culinary.edu

San Francisco State University
1600 Holloway Avenue
San Francisco, CA 94132
Phone: (415) 338-1111
www.sfsu.edu

University of Denver
2199 S. University Boulevard

Denver, CO 80208
Phone: (303) 871-2000
www.du.edu

Western Culinary Institute
921 SW Morrison Street, Suite 400
Portland, OR 97205
Phone: (888) 765-6666
www.wci.edu

Schools in the Midwest
The Cooking and Hospitality Institute of Chicago
361 W Chestnut Street
Chicago, IL 60610
Phone: (877) 828-7772
www.chic.edu

The French Pastry School
226 West Jackson Boulevard
Chicago, IL 60606
Phone: (312) 726-2419
Fax: (312) 726-2446
www.frenchpastryschool.com
e-mail: info@frenchpastryschool.com

The Illinois Institute of Art–Chicago
(Culinary Satellite Location)
180 N. Wabash Avenue
Chicago, IL 60601

Phone: (800) 351-3450
www.ilia.aii.edu

Ivy Tech
50 West Fall Creek Parkway North Drive
Indianapolis, IN 46208-5752
Phone: (888) 489-5463
www.ivytech.edu

Kansas State University
College of Human Ecology
119 Justin Hall
Manhattan, KS 66506
Phone: (785) 532-5500
www.humec.ksu.edu
e-mail: heinfo@humec.ksu.edu

Kendall College
900 N. North Branch Street
Chicago, IL 60622
Phone: (866) 667-3344
www.kendall.edu

Metropolitan Community College
P.O. Box 3777
Omaha, NE 68103-0777
Phone: (800) 228-9553
www.mccneb.edu
e-mail: info@mccneb.edu

Michigan State University

School of Hospitality Business
232 Eppley Center
East Lansing, MI 48824
Phone: (517) 353-9211
www.bus.msu.edu/shb
e-mail: hbusiness@bus.msu.edu

Missouri State University

Hospitality and Restaurant Administration
901 S. National
Springfield, MO 65897
Phone: (417) 836-5136
www.missouristate.edu/acs/HRA%20Home.htm

North Dakota State University

Apparel, Design, Facility and Hospitality Management
Evelyn Morrow Lebedeff Hall 178
Fargo, ND 58105
Phone: (701) 231-8604
Fax: (701) 231-5273
www.ndsu.edu/adfhm/hm/index.htm

Purdue University

College of Consumer and Family Sciences
Department of Hospitality and Tourism Management
West Lafayette, IN 47907
Phone: (765) 494-4600
www.cfs.purdue.edu

University of Missouri–Columbia
Columbia, MO 65211
Phone: (573) 882-4114
http://cafnr.missouri.edu/departments/fse/HRM/Default.asp
e-mail: HRMdept@missouri.edu

Schools in the Southeast
Culinard
Culinary Institute of Virginia College
Birmingham, AL 35209
Phone: (877) 429-2433
www.culinard.com

Florida Culinary Institute (FCI)
2410 Metrocentre Boulevard
West Palm Beach, FL 33407
Phone: (877) 523-7549
Fax: (561) 688-9882
www.floridaculinary.com
e-mail: info@floridaculinary.com

Florida International University
Continuing and Professional Studies (CAPS)
University Park Campus, GL 120
11200 S.W. 8th Street
Miami, FL 33199
Phone: (305) 348-5669
Fax: (305) 348-1561

http://caps.@fiu.edu/credit.htm
e-mail: caps@fiu.edu

George Washington University
Department of Tourism and Hospitality Management
600 21 Street NW
Washington, DC 20052
Phone: (202) 994-6281
www.gwutourism.org

Keiser College
Capital Culinary Institute
1700 Halstead Boulevard, Building 2
Tallahassee, FL 32309
Phone: (877) CHEF-123 or (850) 906-9494
Fax: (850) 906-9497

or

900 S. Babcock Street
Melbourne, FL 32901
Phone: (321) 255-2255
Fax: (321) 725-3766
www.capitalculinaryinstitute.com/culinary.html

Orlando Culinary Academy
8511 Commodity Circle, Suite 100
Orlando, FL 32819
Phone: (866) 622-2433
www.orlandoculinary.com

Stratford University
School of Culinary Arts & Hospitality
Falls Church Campus
7777 Leesburg Pike
Falls Church, VA 22043
Phone: (800) 444-0804

Woodbridge Campus
13576 Minnieville Road
Woodbridge, VA 22192
Phone: (888) 546-1250
www.stratford.edu/?page=home_culinary

University of Central Florida
Rosen College of Hospitality Management
9907 Universal Boulevard
Orlando, FL 32819
Phone: (407) 903-8000
Fax: (407) 903-8105
www.hospitality.ucf.edu
e-mail: hospitality@mail.ucf.edu

Schools in Texas
Culinary Academy of Austin
2823 Hancock Drive
Austin, TX 78731
Phone: (512) 451-5743
Fax: (512) 467-9120

www.culinaryacademyofaustin.com
e-mail: info@culinaryacademyofaustin.com

Texas Culinary Academy
11400 Burnet Road, Suite 2100
Austin, TX 78758
Phone: (512) 837-2665
www.tca.edu

Industry
Organizations

American Beverage Institute
1775 Pennsylvania Avenue NW
Suite 1200
Washington, DC 20006
Phone: (202) 463-7110
www.bacdebate.com

American Culinary Federation
180 Center Place Way
St. Augustine, FL 32095
Phone: (800) 624-9458
Fax: (904) 825-4758
www.acfchefs.org
e-mail: acf@acfchefs.net

Council for Independent Restaurants of America (CIRA)
Don Luria, President CIRA
3500 East Sunrise Drive
Tucson, AZ 85718
Phone: (520) 577-8181
Fax: (520) 577-9015
www.dineoriginals.com
e-mail: CIRAPresident@aol.com

Federation of Dining Room Professionals (FDRP)
1417 Sadler Road #100
Fernandina Beach, FL 32034
Phone: (877) 264-FDRP
Fax: (904) 491-6689
www.fdrp.com
e-mail: info@fdrp.com

The Food Institute
One Broadway
Elmwood Park, NJ 07407
Phone: (201) 791-5570
Fax: (201) 791-5222
www.foodinstitute.com

International Association of Culinary Professionals
304 West Liberty Street, Suite 201
Louisville, KY 40220
Phone: (502) 581-9785

Fax: (502) 589-3602
www.iacp.com
e-mail: iacp@hqtrs.com

International Association for Food Protection
6200 Aurora Avenue, Suite 200W
Des Moines, IA 50322-2864
Phone: (515) 276-3344 or (800) 369-6337
Fax: (515) 276-8655
www.foodprotection.org
e-mail: info@foodprotection.org

The International Council on Hotel, Restaurant and Institutional Education (CHRIE)
2810 North Parham Road, Suite 230
Richmond, VA 23294
Phone: (804) 346-4800
Fax: (804) 346-5009
www.chrie.org

The James Beard Foundation
167 W. 12th Street
New York, NY 10011
Phone: (800) 36-BEARD
www.jamesbeard.org
e-mail: membership@jamesbeard.org

La Chaine de Rotisseurs
Confrérie de la Chaîne des Rôtisseurs

Chaîne House at Fairleigh Dickinson University
285 Madison Avenue
Madison, NJ 07940-1099
Phone: (973) 360-9200
Fax: (973) 360-9330
www.chaineus.org
e-mail: chaine@chaineus.org

National Restaurant Association
1200 17th Street
Washington, DC 20036-3097
Phone: (202) 331-5900
Fax: (202) 331-2429
www.restaurant.org

National Restaurant Association Educational Foundation
175 West Jackson Boulevard, Suite 1500
Chicago, IL 60604-2702
Phone: (800) 765-2122
www.nraef.org
e-mail: info@nraef.org

United States Professional Chefs Association
481 Rio Rancho Boulevard NE
Rio Rancho, NM 87124
Phone: (800) 995-2138
www.uspca.com

Women Chefs and Restaurateurs

304 W. Liberty Street, Suite 201
Louisville, KY 40202
Phone: (877) 927-7787
Fax: (502) 589-3602
www.womenchefs.org

Women's Foodservice Forum

101 N. Wacker Drive, Suite 606
Chicago, IL 60606
Phone: (866) 368-8008
www.womensfoodserviceforum.com
e-mail: info@womensfoodserviceforum.com

Glossary

86. Means an item is unavailable. For example, an expo might call, "We're 86 Prime Rib," which means the restaurant is out of prime rib. Some people also use 86 to reference a customer who is denied service in a particular restaurant.

All day. Used when getting a total count of items at a station. The expo might call out, "I got seven lobsters all day," which means that the cook working the lobster station should have seven lobsters total in the process of preparation.

Alley. The area in the kitchen where the waitstaff can move from one side of the kitchen to the other without interfering with the cooks.

Alley rally. A casual name for a pre-shift meeting with all staff members to discuss specials, goals for the shifts, and other things. It sometimes takes place in the kitchen alley, hence the name.

Auction. A food runner or server stands at the table with dishes in hand, says the name of the dish and waits for the guest to tell her who ordered it. In some restaurants, this practice is not permitted.

Back of the house (BOH). The area in the kitchen that guests don't usually see, like the kitchen, storage areas, and offices.

Behind you. A phrase used as you walk behind someone. It lets someone who can't see you know you're there so they won't turn around while you (or they) are carrying hot soup, sharp knives, or a stack of glasses on a tray.

Bev nap. Short for beverage napkin. Small square cocktail napkins.

Blue hairs. Derogatory term for elderly ladies.

Blue laws. Laws that restrict sales of certain goods or restrict certain activities on Sunday. The laws vary from state to state and most often affect the sale of alcohol.

BOH. Acronym for Back of the House. Only written, never spoken.

Breakage. The breaking of smallwares like plates, glasses, other breakable items. Restaurants watch breakage to control costs and maintain safety.

Bucket of steam. As an initiate right, BOH employees sometimes ask new employees to find nonexistent items like a bucket of steam.

Bug night. A set night (usually monthly) when the restaurant prepares for a regular visit from the exterminator. Employees make extra preparations, like protecting dried goods normally left out, and covering up smallwares to ensure that no toxins come into contact with something a guest might receive.

Buried. To be extremely busy. "The grill is buried" means the grill is busy.

Bus tub buffet. Eating food from diners' discarded plates.

Busser. A restaurant employee who clears and resets tables.

C:Server. A note typed into the POS to alert the kitchen that the dish has some special requirements. They should see (C:) the server before preparing the dish. Most restaurants expect employees to use this note in emergencies only because standard modifications to a dish (hold the onions, for example) can be entered directly into the system.

Call ahead seating. A system that allows diners to call the restaurant ahead of time to place their names on the waiting list.

Call back. A request to repeat the order to the expo. Expos use this technique to ensure that a station has all the correct items in process. Also called an echo.

Campers. Guests that sit at a table for a long time.

Check back, check down. A system used in casual restaurants for getting a check to the guest. When the server checks back after the guests receive their food, he also drops off the check. If the guest later chooses to have additional menu items, the server retrieves the check, then drops the new revised check.

Concept. The whole package of the restaurant, its food, ambiance, décor, etc. Sometimes called a restaurant's "theme."

Cooler. A refrigerator.

Count. The number of guests.

Cover. A guest. Restaurants keep track of how many covers they do during a day part, day, week, and so on.

Cremate. To burn something.

Cut. To end an employee's shift as business levels taper off. Also called "phasing."

Day part. Another way to refer to the meal period a restaurant serves. Breakfast is a day part, lunch is a day part and so on. Also known as a day period, or dining period.

Day period. See *day part.*

Dead. 1) Not busy, as in "The restaurant is dead tonight." 2) Food that's past it's prime and is no longer servable.

Deuce. A party of two, or a table that seats two people.

Dine & dash. Leaving without paying the check. See also walk-out.

Dining periods. See *day part.*

Dish pit. The dishwashing area.

Double. Working two meal periods back to back.

Double-seat. Seating two parties in the same section in rapid succession.

Double tip. Adding a tip on top of a required tip. If a restaurant requires a 15 percent gratuity for large parties, that amount will have been placed on the check when it's presented. Some parties add an additional tip to the bill.

Douche. The process of hosing down the kitchen at the end of the night.

Douse it. Cover something in sauce.

Down. Describes the condition of having a party seated in a particular section. One server might say to another, "Your 6-top is down," meaning "You have a party sitting at your 6-top."

Dragging. When a dish or part of a dish isn't ready with the rest of the food for a single part, an expo says it's dragging. It's an indication to take the food that's ready to the table and the "dragging" item will be sent separately. In some styles of service, fine dining for example, this is not permitted. In others, it's common.

Drop. A command that alerts a line cook to start cooking or "fire" an item that is immersed, usually either in water (pasta or lobster for example) or hot oil (like fries).

Dying. The condition that occurs shortly before being dead. See also *dead*.

Echo. Repeat the order to the expo immediately after he calls it the first time. See also *call back*.

Employee meal. A discount offered to employees on food purchased before or after their shifts.

Expeditor ("Expo"). The liaison between the BOH and the FOH. The expo receives the orders and coordinates their preparation by communicating with all the cooks on the line. She also communicates with the FOH as necessary.

Eye in the Sky. The security cameras in a restaurant.

Family meal. Some restaurants serve this meal to employees between the lunch and dinner periods. They offer one meal, and everyone eats together.

Fast casual. A style of service that offers quick, quality food with fresh ingredients, in a wide range of flavors, served in a very informal environment.

FIFO. An acronym for "First In First Out," meaning the oldest products (those that were first in the cooler) should be used first (first out). It's a standard system for rotating perishables and minimizing waste.

Fire. A command the expo gives a cook when it's time to begin preparing a dish.

Fish file. A pull-out refrigerated drawer that holds delicate seafood items until they are ready to be fired.

FNG. A borrowed military term, meaning F*&#@* New Guy/Girl.

FOH. Acronym for Front of the House. Only written, never spoken.

Food runner. An employee who takes food from the kitchen to diners as it's ready.

Four-top. A party of four or a table that seats four people.

Franchise. A license to sell a restaurant's food, use its brand identity, look and feel, and other equity. Some restaurants are run as franchises, allowing many people to open many restaurants in many different locations and still offer consistent menus, service, and experiences.

Front of the house (FOH). The area of the restaurant where guests typically go. The dining room, bar, lobby and restrooms are all part of the front of the house.

FUBAR. A borrowed military acronym, meaning F*&#@* Up Beyond All Recognition. It often describes a large party that's gone horribly wrong or the physical state of the restaurant after a busy shift.

Gone. Describes food that's dead. See *dead*.

Got time to lean. Short for the rhyme "If you got time to lean, you got time to clean," meaning that there's always something to do (or clean) in a restaurant, so you shouldn't just be standing around or leaning on the counter.

Grease trap. A fixture in plumbing required in restaurant floor drains to catch much of the grease, oil, and other contaminants generated before they can go into the sewage system. They need to be cleaned regularly, and it's a messy job. Often cleaning them is the least desired job in the kitchen.

Greeter. An employee who makes contact with diners as they walk in the door of the restaurant. They usually get the menus and seat the guests at their tables. See also *Host/Hostess*.

Growl. The long, springing faucet in the dishwashing area, used to rinse dishes before they're placed in the mechanical dishwasher and sanitizer.

Guest. A customer.

Hockey puck. A piece of food that is very burned.

Hold time. Describes how long a dish or food can sit after being prepared before it's dead. Often used in catering.

Hopping. Busy, with a good connotation.

Hostess, Host. See *Greeter*.

Hot behind. A phrase you say as you walk behind someone with something very hot. See also *behind you*.

Hotel pan. A large shallow metal pan that holds food in a steam table. Smaller sizes of these pans are called "half pans," "third pans," and so on, depending on how big they are in relation to the full size hotel pan.

In the weeds. Extremely busy, with a bad connotation. See *weeded*.

Incentive. A contest used by managers to encourage sales of a particular item. A manager may offer a free bottle of wine to the employee who sells the most wine during a shift.

Jumping. Busy, with a good connotation.

Line. The area of the kitchen where food is prepared. This area is usually separate from the prep area in a kitchen.

Line cook. A cook that works on the line.

Line up. A preshift meeting used to make sure everyone has all the information they need to work together during the shift. Also called premeal or alley rally in some restaurants.

Maitre'd. A manager who runs the podium and coordinates the seating of guests coming into the restaurant. Used only in fine dining.

Meal periods. See *day part*.

No call/No show. Someone (usually an employee or a reservation) that doesn't show up at the appointed time and doesn't call with an explanation.

Nuke. The action of cooking something in the microwave.

On a rail. See *on the fly*.

On the fly. To need something quickly. It's sometimes altered as in, "I need it flying." See also *on a rail* and *on the hop*.

On the hop. See *on the fly*.

Order up. An order is ready to take to the table.

Party. A group of guests sitting at the same table.

Phase. See *cut*.

Pittsburgh. A term used to describe meat that's burned on the outside, but rare on the inside.

Poppy seed splitter. As an initiate right, BOH employees sometimes ask new employees to find nonexistent items like a poppy seed splitter.

POS system. An acronym for point of sale system. It's the computer system servers use to input orders, process payments, and so on.

Pour size. The amount of liquor used in a cocktail.

Pre-meal. See *line up*.

Prebus. The strategy of removing as many items as possible from a table while a guest is still seated. Ideally when a guest leaves the table, only the table setup and the last glasses remain. Once the guest leaves, it's much quicker to clean and reset the table if it's prebussed.

Prep cook. A cook who works to prepare many components of dishes ahead of time.

Prep kitchen. A separate area in the kitchen where large quantities of stock ingredients are prepared preshift.

Q Factor. A financial factor that restaurants use when pricing and figuring costs that account for the costs of many paper products (like straws, napkins, paper bags) and to-go condiments (like ketchup).

QSR. Quick Service Restaurant, aka, fast food restaurant.

Quote. The time "quoted" to guests for how long they can expect to wait for a table.

Reach-in. Small refrigerator that you "reach-in" to.

Rollup. A set of silverware rolled in a large dinner napkin.

Runner. See *food runner*.

Running. Asking the server for one thing at a time, so the server is "running" back and forth.

Rush. The busy period during a shift.

SOS. Sauce on the side.

Sam and Ella. A term of endearment for the common food-borne bacteria, salmonella.

Sanitizer. Chemical used to kill bacteria and other germs on surfaces (like tables, counters, cutting boards), knives, and on everything that goes through the dishwasher.

Sat/seat. To bring a party to a table. Usually done by a greeter.

Section. A group of tables assigned to a specific server during a shift. Sometimes called a station.

Sell. To put a completed food order ticket in the window with all of the food, ready to be delivered to the table.

Server. A member of the waitstaff.

Shorted. Describes missing items from a party's food order. It implies that a mistake of some sort was made. Note that if you know an item is dragging, then you weren't shorted.

Sidework. Work done by FOH employees each shift to ready the restaurant for the next shift. It usually includes cleaning (wiping down your tables and sweeping your section), restocking things (like ice, glassware, or plates), or rolling silverware.

Skate. Leaving without finishing assigned duties, especially sidework.

Slammed. Being busy. Not as negative as "weeded."

Smallwares. Smaller pieces of nonmechanical equipment like plates, glasses, ramekins, and coffee cups.

Snake. Taking a table that doesn't belong to you.

Sommelier. A wine specialist.

Spindle. A pointy metal stake in the window used to discard tickets for food orders taken to tables.

Split. 1) Working a shift, leaving, then coming back to work for a second shift. Similar to a double. 2) Sharing a dish, as in "we're going to split the fettuccine."

Station or section. 1) In the BOH, it describes an area on the line that produces dishes with a particular preparation method. The grill is a station, the pantry is a station, and so on. 2) Sometimes used in the FOH to describe the tables assigned to a server.

Steam table. Works like a huge chafing dish. It holds many hotel pans full of prepared foods and keeps them warm until they are ready to use.

Stiffed. Receiving no tip from a table.

Still moving. Describes a dish that's too rare.

Store. Used instead of the term "restaurant" in a corporate environment. A district manager may be in charge of seven to ten different stores (restaurants).

Stretch it. Describes a situation in which a cook may be running out of an item (usually a sauce or side dish), and he adds something else to make the quantity last "or stretch" for the dishes that still need to be plated.

Table setup. Whatever stuff is on each table. A setup might include salt and pepper, sugar, ketchup, and a drink menu.

The man. The health inspector.

The pit. The dishwashing area.

Thin to win. Similar to "stretching," but this term is usually only used with liquids. In an emergency, a cook may add a little more oil to a salad dressing to make sure she has enough.

Ticket. The paper that conveys a table's order to the person (usually the expo or bartender) making the order.

Tips. Stands for "To ensure prompt service." Guests tip a server based on the level of service. In the United States, a standard tip is 15 to 20 percent.

Tip out. The practice of giving support staff (like bussers, food runners, and service bartenders) a portion of tips based on their service to the waitstaff.

Top. Used to describe the number of people at a table. Also used to describe the size of the actual table. A section may be made up of two four-tops and two two-tops, for example.

Toque. Tall white hat worn by a chef.

Triple-seat. Seating three parties in the same section in rapid succession.

Turn. A change of parties at a table. Servers turn the table after one party finishes its meal, the table is cleaned, and another party sits down.

Turn and burn. Cycling guests through a restaurant quickly.

Upsell. Sell more expensive or additional items that enhance the guest's experience at the restaurant.

Waitstaff. Employees in the restaurant who wait on customers, take orders, and bring items as needed. Also called *servers*.

Waiter/Waitress. A member of the waitstaff.

Waitron. A disparaging term for server or waiter.

Walk-in. Large refrigerated "rooms" that you can walk into.

Walk-in microwave. As an initiate right, BOH employees sometimes ask new employees to find non-existent items like a walk-in microwave.

Walkout. Customer who leaves without paying a check.

Weeded. Being too busy. Usually happens in the middle of a rush.

Window. The space in the kitchen where the BOH staff places food when it's ready to be served to customers.

Working. A term usually used by the expo to mean, "The food is being prepared."

Working hard. A term usually used by the expo to mean, "The food is being prepared, and don't ask me again."

Index